D1329910

PROLEGOMENA

TO

AN IDEALIST THEORY OF KNOWLEDGE

MACMILLAN AND CO., Limited
LONDON · BOMBAY · CALCUTTA · MADRAS
MELBOURNE

THE MACMILLAN COMPANY
NEW YORK · BOSTON · CHICAGO
DALLAS · SAN FRANCISCO

THE MACMILLAN CO. OF CANADA, Ltd.
TORONTO

PROLEGOMENA
TO
AN IDEALIST THEORY
OF KNOWLEDGE

BY

NORMAN KEMP SMITH
D.PHIL., LL.D.

PROFESSOR OF LOGIC AND METAPHYSICS IN THE UNIVERSITY OF EDINBURGH

MACMILLAN AND CO., LIMITED
ST. MARTIN'S STREET, LONDON
1924

COPYRIGHT

TO

S. ALEXANDER

AND

G. F. STOUT

IN

GRATEFUL INDEBTEDNESS

PREFACE

THIS volume is the outcome of material which I prepared for use as Mill's Lecturer in Philosophy at the University of California, January to May, 1923. In it I have endeavoured to carry through an enterprise which I have long had in mind, namely, the formulation of an idealist theory of knowledge on realist lines.

In the late 'nineties I had come to be interested in Malebranche's philosophy, and thereby was fortunate in finding a bond of common interest with Mr. S. Alexander, to whom the realist features in Malebranche's teaching had made special appeal. Mr. Alexander then, happily, directed my attention to the writings of Avenarius. I had also become acquainted with M. Bergson's *Les Données immédiates de la Conscience* and *Matière et Mémoire*; and at that time I believed myself able to trace certain realist tendencies common to him and to Avenarius. Some paragraphs from articles in the *Philosophical Review* (1908) and *Journal of Philosophy* (1912), expressive of my attitude in these years, I have, by permission of the editors, incorporated, with a few changes, in the present volume. Since 1912, however, my views have undergone very radical alteration, though still in the direction of realism and without departure from the idealist standpoint. In this recasting of my views I have been greatly aided by study of the works of Baron von Hügel.

Though I cannot follow on the lines travelled by M. Bergson, his writings have left their influence, and I have especially profited by his analysis of time, and by the somewhat kindred teaching of Mr. Whitehead in this regard. Otherwise, among present-day writers, my chief debts, in questions bearing directly on the theory of knowledge, are to Mr. Alexander and to Mr. Stout.

Mr. Broad's *Scientific Thought* (1923) only came into my hands while I was making a final revision of these pages. In Chapters IV. and V. I have taken account of some of his discussions.

I am also under many personal obligations in the actual preparation of this volume. Mr. Stout has read through my manuscript, in its earlier form ; and I have immensely benefited by his criticisms, perhaps not least in those cases in which I have still ventured to differ from him. My friend, Mr. A. A. Bowman of Princeton University, has done me a similar service. My colleague, Mr. John Anderson, has read the entire proofs. Owing to his watchful care and very searching criticisms, the volume is much less imperfect than it would otherwise have been.

NORMAN KEMP SMITH.

EDINBURGH,
February 1924.

CONTENTS

CHAPTER I

INTRODUCTORY

CHAPTER II

THE DOCTRINE OF REPRESENTATIVE PERCEPTION

CHAPTER III

ARGUMENT IN SUPPORT OF THE DOCTRINE OF REPRESENTATIVE PERCEPTION

xi

CHAPTER IV

ARGUMENT IN CRITICISM OF THE DOCTRINE OF REPRESENTATIVE PERCEPTION

CHAPTER V

THE NATURE AND FUNCTIONS OF THE SENSA

CHAPTER VI

THE PRESENTATIONAL CONTINUUM

CHAPTER VII
THE CATEGORIES

CHAPTER VIII
SENSE AND INTUITION

CHAPTER IX
CONCLUSIONS

CHAPTER I

INTRODUCTORY

(i.) IDEALISM AND NATURALISM

THE meanings attached to the term ' idealism ' are so numerous and so conflicting that I have found it convenient to use it in a very wide sense, as covering all those philosophies which agree in maintaining that spiritual values have a determining voice in the ordering of the Universe. The alternative position, as represented by what is now most usually entitled ' naturalism,' is that these values emerge, and begin to vindicate their reality, only at some late stage in a process of evolution. This may not, perhaps, be a wholly satisfactory method of distinguishing between these opposite types of philosophy, but will at least suffice to indicate the very general meaning in which I shall employ the two terms.

On first thoughts, the possible methods of upholding idealism may well appear, broadly stated, to be only two in number. Either we may strive to demonstrate that matter is so opposite in nature to mind that it is patently incapable of generating or of accounting for it; or we may profess to demonstrate that matter, as dependent on consciousness, itself bears witness to the reality of mind. The history of philosophy would seem, however, to show that the former method, while possibly tenable in some other formulation than any which has hitherto been given of it, presupposes a more complete knowledge both of mind and of matter than we can yet rightly claim to possess, and that the latter method, though representing the standpoint of so acute and distinguished a thinker as Berkeley, and in some degree also of Kant, has failed to make good its fundamental contention, that matter is mind-dependent.

The limitations of these two methods crop out in the very unsatisfactory interpretations of Nature to which they respectively commit us.   On the one view, Nature is supposed to be adequately envisaged in terms of Cartesian principles, as revised by Newton.   Its components, it is asserted, are as incapable of life as of consciousness, and are therefore exhaustively known in terms of those mechanical properties which in all their reactions, even in those that are simplest, they unvaryingly display.   Nature, thus regarded, is in its fundamentals non-mysterious; it can conceal no undisclosed secrets, save only in regard to the special detail of its mechanical complexities.   Berkeley, though arguing on the opposite, alternative lines, arrives at a somewhat similar conclusion.   On his view, also, the natural world is deprived of all that is mysterious to the human understanding.   Sense-experience, Berkeley teaches, has the intelligibility of a language whose conventions are one and all determined by a Spirit akin to our own, and it discourses, not of the splendours and dynamic potencies of an independent Order, but solely of the decisions of God in the arranging of the components of immediate experience.   The surface of Nature is, so to speak, its whole reality.   For though Nature is always prolonged, alike as regards outer shapes and so-called inner parts, in other actual or possible experiences, it consists exhaustively in that as which it is directly apprehended, namely, in sensations. The more general laws of their fundamental coexistences and sequences remain for discovery through scientific inquiry; but to the end it is in sensations, externally and arbitrarily conjoined, that Nature consists.

One main thesis of this volume will be that idealism is indeed precariously founded, if it seeks to establish itself by either of the above methods. Nature has a stubborn independence and an adaptiveness of behaviour which rule out any description of it either, on the one hand, as the creature, or, on the other hand, as the opposite of mind; it exhibits an efficacy and an initiative, a resourcefulness and, in the organic realm, a wilfulness not wholly without analogy to the activities of the self. And if we further recognise, as seemingly we must, that among Nature's constituents are those qualitatively varying entities, sound, colour, and the like, which hitherto, owing to lack of any discoverable connection between them and their physical basis, have usually been classed as mental in origin, we should be under no misapprehension as to the extent to which Nature still withholds itself from our grasp; even as regards ultimate constituents, it must, we may presume, contain very much more than it has yet revealed to us. If spiritual values, as interpreted in terms of idealist philosophy, have so little hold on reality as to be threatened by a Nature thus envisaged, naturalism, I should feel constrained to believe, is not unlikely to prove their more helpful ally, and to be alone worthy of our allegiance.

Accordingly I shall maintain that what is most truly distinctive in idealism is its central contention, that spiritual values can be credited as operating on a more than planetary, that is, on a *cosmic* scale. Should this contention have to be given up, the only sort of ' idealism ' which would then remain would no longer be distinguishable from some at least of the naturalistic philosophies. For these are certainly no less insistent in maintaining that the criteria yielded by spiritual values exercise a predominating influence in *human* affairs. If we hold at all to the opposition between idealism and naturalism, we must recognise it as being the distinction between a religious and a secularist view of life; and the consequences which follow, whether practical or con- templative, according as the one or the other is adopted, will be of the kind which these terms suggest.

(ii.) IDEALISM AND SUBJECTIVISM

I further distinguish between subjectivism and idealism. Subjectivism and realism are, I should hold, methods and points of view to which both idealism and naturalism may, as seems good, find reason to resort. Certainly, in the past, neither ideal- ism nor naturalism has exclusively committed itself, save in this or that individual representative, either to subjectivist or to realist principles. Frequently the two types of principle supplement one another— whether consistently or not is a further question— within the same philosophy.

Subjectivism is itself, of course, a term which can be employed in a great variety of quite legitimate meanings. I prefer to employ it, save where indica- tion is given to the contrary, in its widest possible connotation. I shall mean by it any view which either, as with Descartes, advocates a doctrine of representative perception, or, as with Berkeley and his followers, endeavours to interpret ' real ' objects as being mind-dependent. For, however widely Descartes and Berkeley may diverge in their ultimate results, yet common to both, as I shall endeavour to show, are certain fundamental assumptions, inconsistent with any genuinely realist interpretation of human experience. That, for instance, Berkeley's ' real ' objects are not the objects believed in by ordinary consciousness, but are simply Descartes' representative ideas masquerading in place of their betters, would, as already suggested, seem to be shown by their admitted causal inefficacy, and by their consequent incapacity to constitute any other Order than that of a body of conventionally agreed symbols, analogous to those of human speech.

So deeply, however, have subjectivist ways of thinking entrenched themselves in general thought, ever since the seventeenth century, that the naturalistic position has hitherto, almost invariably, been made to rest upon similar foundations. For though, of course, mainly based upon data accumulated in the special sciences, it has, as regards its modes of statement, and many of its chief arguments, been reached through Hume, by way of Berkeley, and has therefore consisted—Herbert Spencer and Huxley are here typical protagonists of nineteenth-century naturalism —in a very strange amalgam of subjectivism plus mechanism. The world is represented as being made up of two parallel but independent series, states of immediate experience on the one hand, mechanical processes on the other. The position may be supplemented by certain agnostic pronouncements regarding an unknowable reality underlying and presumably co-ordinating the separate series; but on the specific teaching, and the prevailing temper of these philosophies, such supplementary dicta are almost entirely without effect.

The assertion that the two series run their courses in complete independence, without discernible connection, save only that of temporal coincidence, is plainly incompatible with our having knowledge of them both. For all the knowledge there is must, it is alleged, be conveyed, not by any process outside the two series, and postulated *ad hoc*—that, in the view of these thinkers, would be to rival idealism at its worst—but by that one of the two series which is made up of the immediate experiences. This, however, is precisely what, on the principles maintained by Spencer and Huxley, cannot, consistently, be allowed as possible. For they would then be postulating a type of transcendence — the immediate experiences yielding knowledge of the mechanical processes—which would contrast with the only forms of physical happening that they are willing to recognise, and which could not, therefore, be harmonised — so, in other connections, they have themselves argued—with any strictly naturalistic scheme.

Recently, however, this long-accepted assumption has been boldly challenged, and a massive body of non-subjectivist teaching erected, most notably by Mr. S. Alexander, and in some degree also by Mr. Whitehead, upon genuinely naturalistic foundations. Why, they ask, this refusal to accept, as compatible with naturalistic categories, any mode or form of transcendence? Is not transcendence a process which in general type is co-extensive with physical nature? What is causal action if not transcendence by the

agent of its own private limits; and what is causal
affection if not response by the patient to what lies
beyond itself ?[1]   If causal action be first interpreted,
in terms of a subjectivist philosophy, in the manner
of Hume, it will, of course, yield no analogy in support
of a self-transcending awareness; but if it be interpreted realistically, the situation is quite otherwise,
and new possibilities open to our view.   This is a
lesson by which idealists may well profit; and I have
sought to do so in the present volume.   I have been
greatly assisted by many of the new doctrines which
Mr. Alexander has developed with striking originality,
especially as regards our apprehension of space and of
past time.   Their author must, however, I fear, deplore
what he may well regard as my perverse twisting of
correct arguments to wrong conclusions.

[1] Cf. Alexander, *Space, Time and Deity*, vol. ii. pp. 81-2: "The first and
simplest relation between finite existences . . . is their comprescence within one
Space-Time of which all alike are differentiations.   The behaviour of finites
to one another in this relation of comprescence is determined by the character
of the finites.   The plant lives, grows, and breathes, and twines around a
stick.   The material body resists, or falls, or sounds when struck, or emits
light when touched by the sun.   The mind knows.   Mind is for us the
highest order of finite empirical existent. . . . Cognition, then, instead of
being a unique relation, is nothing but an instance of the simplest and most
universal of all relations."   " Colour is revealed to me because I have eyes,
while it is not revealed to the plant as colour but only as something which
affects the chlorophyll in the plant.   Or I hear the sound of the tuning-fork,
but the sound may be revealed to a tuning-fork which it sets in sympathetic
vibration only as a vibratory material affection of the source in question "
(*op. cit.* ii. p. 100).   Cf. also Whitehead, *The Concept of Nature*, p. 145:
" Science and philosophy have been apt to entangle themselves in a simple-
minded theory that an object is at one place at any definite time, and is in
no sense anywhere else.   This is in fact the attitude of commonsense thought,
though it is not the attitude of language which is naïvely expressing the facts
of experience.   Every other sentence in a work of literature which is endeavouring truly to interpret the facts of experience expresses differences in
surrounding events due to the presence of some object.   An object is
ingredient throughout its neighbourhood, and its neighbourhood is indefinite."

(iii.) THE REQUIREMENTS OF IDEALISM

Idealists, as the reading of history would seem to show, have been apt to overreach themselves, and to weaken the force of their own better arguments, by attempting to prove very much more than the available data can justly be expected to yield. Since the time of Kant, and largely through his influence, the uncompromising Berkeleian thesis, that ' material ' Nature is mind-dependent, has, indeed, been displaced by what, initially at least, is the more modest, though also usually much less definite, claim that Mind and Nature stand in relations of mutual implication. But even this claim has frequently been urged, especially by thinkers of the Hegelian type, in forms much more ambitious than the needs of an idealist orientation towards life and towards the Universe would seem to demand.

Thus Mr. F. H. Bradley and Mr. Bernard Bosanquet have maintained that everything is *experience*. When this useful term, with its twofold meaning—experiencing and the experienced—is thus employed in this very wide sense, these writers are, it is true, enabled to evade many of the chief controversies which centre round the names of Descartes, Berkeley, Hume, and Kant; but they are in position to do so only because they have restricted themselves to those considerations of *logical* implication whereby self and not-self, subject and object, Mind and Nature are supposed to demonstrate their inseparable, mutual interconnection. But by such methods they have never yet succeeded in giving, in terms of their own standpoint, any really satisfactory account of that other very different, and yet surely no less important type of connection in which physical existences exhibit *causal* efficacy, and in which physical and physiological processes *actively* condition our inner experiences and the apprehension of the outer world that goes there-with. Such a standpoint also constrains its adherents to the acceptance of an Absolute; and this Absolute is so far from yielding—so at least it would seem to those who are unable to follow on these lines—a satis-factory synoptic outlook, that, on the contrary, alike as regards Nature and as regards the facts of human experience, it blurs the significance and diminishes the importance of just those distinctions and values which are of chief concern to us, and which it itself professes to have safeguarded and upheld.

May not, then, the analysis of experience and its philosophical interpretation carry us sufficiently far to discern certain ultimate alternatives, bearing upon the meaning of life and of the Universe, and even perhaps to find grounds adequate for deciding between these alternatives, and yet not enable us to have understand-ing, say, in the difficult issue as to the relation of mind and matter, how the chosen alternative works itself out? May we not be in position to give an answer decisive of our attitude towards naturalism and idealism respectively, and yet not be called upon to determine more than a few main consequences that follow from this choice? The many other possible questions, if really relevant to human requirements, presumably await answer, either through the advance of scientific inquiry or, when that remains impracticable, by the less strictly theoretical, and for that reason so much more adventurous and immensely more costly methods of human trial and failure.

These introductory remarks are perhaps in some

degree misleading, in that they suggest a larger canvas than I have attempted to handle in this volume.   They may, however, be helpful as indicating the kind of position towards which I have believed myself to be working.

(iv.) OUTLINE OF ARGUMENT

Coming now to the special, more detailed, character of my argument, it may be outlined as follows.   Since time and space are as real as the revolutions of the planets and the growth of trees, to regard them as being subjective is to reduce external Nature to the level of an illusory appearance.   In order, therefore, to uphold a realist view of Nature, I shall contend that time and space are independently real, that as such they disclose themselves directly to the mind, that in so doing they prescribe certain categories which are involved in their apprehension, and that these categories equip the mind for discerning those ideals which constrain it to the pursuit of science and philosophy.

Time and space do not, however, reveal themselves to us save in terms of sensa.   Consequently, in the development of a realist view of Nature we are faced, at the start, by a choice of routes.   Either we may proceed by regarding the sensuous features—colour, sound, heat and cold, etc.—as being qualities inherent in the independently existing physical bodies, or we may interpret them as being events which demand for their occurrence supplementary conditions of a physiological character.

Each view has its own difficulties; and each, on the other hand, has certain initial advantages.   My choice is for the latter alternative.   The sensa, I shall argue, first emerge together with life and consciousness, as necessary for the effective functioning of animal organisms. The physical world is, as the positive sciences demonstrate, so extraordinarily complicated that anything approaching complete experience of it, or even at any moment of any one part of it, far exceeds the utmost capacities of the human, no less than of the animal, mind. Indeed, since Nature, and each object in Nature, contains so many features which from the point of view of our practical needs are entirely irrelevant, such exhaustive experience, even if possible, would so bewilder and distract the mind that its primary function, viz. the initiating and directing of bodily movements, could not be efficiently exercised. Such consciousness would be self-defeating. If, therefore, practical adaptation is to be achieved, Nature, in the processes which condition its being experienced, must be adjusted to the dimensions of the animal and human consciousness. And in this reduction there are three main requirements which have to be fulfilled: first, that the world be simplified by omission of all but a small selection of its multitudinous detail; secondly, that nothing directly relevant to the instinctive and other practical needs of the animal concerned be left out of account; and, thirdly, that the features retained be apprehended with all the definiteness and precision required for initiating, and on the higher levels for controlling, the necessary manipulative and defensive movements. These requirements have been successfully met by Nature's ingenious device of the 'secondary qualities.' How complete, for instance, is the transformation when the millions of violently energetic, discrete entities which compose a drop of water are apprehended as a uniform whitish-coloured globule of

seemingly continuous and quiescent matter; and yet
for the purposes of practical life how convenient, and
how entirely adequate!   There is omission, but no
lack of definiteness; there are quite radical alterations,
but none which do not contribute to rapidity and
effectiveness of mental and bodily response.   How
otherwise, in the human domain, could the manual
and the fine arts, which demand the apprehension of
large-scale but none the less subtle and delicate
differences of texture and design, ever have become
possible?   All art is at once selective and creative,
employing the methods of omission in the attainment
of new and quite positive ends.   For such creative
renderings of the otherwise existent, Nature has set
the pattern in its manner of disclosing itself to the
animal and human mind.

Objects, as thus sensuously apprehended, are public
existences.   For though the sensory perspective in
which they are experienced is peculiar to each observer,
we do not have to regard it as subjective, but only as
private.   The uniqueness does not come about through
relation to ' mind '; it is determined by the temporal
and spatial standpoint of the individual and by the
physical and physiological complexities thereby brought
into play.   By discounting the illusions thus generated
—and the illusions, owing to the exclusively objective
character of their conditions, themselves supply the
data adequate for their correction—we can arrive at
a fuller knowledge of the independently real.   Even
the sensa themselves, inasmuch as they are private
without being subjective, can be defined in non-
personal terms, namely, as items integral to an Order
which is much too enigmatic in character, and too
varied in the types of its manifold constituents, to be

adequately envisaged in any purely mechanical terms. The absence of any discoverable connection, save that of a quantitative concomitance, between the sensa on the one hand and their physical and physiological conditions on the other, points, we may presume, to intervening reaches and types of existence to which we have no present means of penetration. Independent Nature is not less, but more, than it is experienced as being.

As we shall find, this view of the sensa is defensible only if it can be maintained that in their intrinsic nature they do not involve what it is now usual to entitle 'extensity.' Accordingly, one of my chief difficulties will be to justify the contention that space is not apprehended *through* sensa, but *in terms of* them.

My general thesis is thus twofold: first, that time, space, and the categories are directly apprehended as constituent of the natural world; and, secondly, that the sensa exist not as 'qualities' but as 'events,' and have a quite definite *biological* function, that of defining the perspective necessary for the purposes of practical adaptation. These positions I endeavour to combine —a difficult task, and how far I am successful the reader must judge—with an entire rejection of the doctrine of representative perception, alike in its earlier, historical, and in its present-day forms. This is why I prepare the ground for the constructive part of my argument by devoting the next three chapters to examination and criticism of that doctrine. While so doing, I also find the opportunity of defining the essentially practical, non-theoretical character of sense-perception, and so of presenting the data upon which my view of the sensa is chiefly based.

The two fundamental tenets, which thus together

form my main thesis, rest on very different considerations, and each calls for separate proof. None the less, they themselves agree in two respects. In the first place, both postulate the possibility of direct, face-to-face apprehension. For though I allege that space is apprehended only in terms of sensa, not through them, I desire to maintain that both space and colour are immediately apprehended. Any other view is surely untenable! How could we hope to *advance* to a knowledge of either in the absence of direct acquaintance? Then, secondly, both tenets rest on the assumption—borne out, I should contend, by all that is most fundamental in our experience—that from start to finish, alike in sense-experience and in knowledge generally, the initiative, and the really controlling forces, come from without. Consider, for instance, Nature's mode of revealing to us the qualitatively varying sensa—in all regards the most enchanting, in some regards the most enigmatic, of its manifold aspects. How exuberant the *creativeness*, and how elaborate the *indirectness*, with which Nature has proceeded in preparing for us the physiological conditions of such sensory experience! And yet how direct, how immediately face-to-face a mode of apprehension this type of sensory experience proves itself to be! As I shall endeavour to show, Nature is no less continuously self-revealing in our other modes of apprehension. Through its temporal and spatial features it imposes upon the mind the use of certain categories, and through these categories the recognition of certain intellectual ideals; in our scientific pursuits we are still the children of Nature, acting under its tutelage and inspired by its communications.

These positions, I need hardly say, do not differ

from other methods of dealing with the problems of knowledge in being free from difficulties. But, as I shall contend, they harmonise better with what must be a first requirement in any satisfactory philosophy which is not avowedly sceptical and which is also realist in intention, namely, that they justify us in believing that Nature is an independent Order, and that alike through the seeming contingencies of sense-experience and through the purposive activities of our discursive thinking, it is educating us into an ever-fuller knowledge of itself. Already it has contrived to secure for us the emergence of scientific insight, and that out of a type of sensory experience which, in its biological origins, is determined in all its features by practical needs. In the realm of *knowledge*, Nature has thus proved to be a very sufficient Providence, a veritable Fairy Godmother with magical powers; our task is to follow on the lines which she prescribes.

CHAPTER II

THE DOCTRINE OF REPRESENTATIVE PERCEPTION

THE doctrine of representative perception as formulated
by Descartes has exercised, from the seventeenth
century onwards, so overwhelming an influence upon
all subsequent philosophical thinking, and in one form
or another still has so many adherents, that it is
advisable that we should consider it before proceeding.
Indeed, so universal has been its influence, in Kant and
his successors, hardly less than in Berkeley and Hume,
in Spinoza and Leibniz, that present-day writers almost
invariably define their respective positions in terms
either of their partial agreement, or of their total
disagreement, with it. The doctrine itself, in turn,
can best be understood by contrast with the standpoint
of ordinary consciousness.

(i.) THE ATTITUDE OF ORDINARY CONSCIOUSNESS

The attitude of the man in the street, and of all of
us in our unsophisticated moments, would probably
not be misrepresented if stated somewhat as follows.
We seem to ourselves to look out through our eyes,
and to have an immediate face-to-face apprehension of
objects and other selves outside and around us. Just
as we can look out through a window, and see the
landscape as it lies there outside the window, so we

seem to look out through the eyes, and to have direct experience of an independently existing world.   But certain quite elementary facts, brought to light by the sciences of physics and physiology, suffice to show that in adopting this attitude we are suffering from an illusion.   The eyes are not exits, but always only entrances.   They are not windows through which the mind can look out, but channels through which nerve-currents pass into the brain.   It is no more possible to look through the eyes than it is to look through a stone wall.   The front of the eye, the pupil, is, it is true, transparent; but the most essential part of the eye, the retina, is opaque.   What really happens would seem, indeed, to be directly contrary to what is being assumed.   Light falling upon the object is reflected to the eye.   Passing in through the pupil, and focussed by the lens, it causes chemical changes in the retina. These chemical changes, in turn, stimulate the optic nerve, and so give rise to nerve-currents which pass to the ' visual area ' in the occipital lobes of the cerebral hemispheres.   In connection with the brain-processes thus aroused there emerge those experiences for which we are seeking to account.

So far there is general agreement.   No one questions that these facts, bearing on the processes involved in vision, have been more or less conclusively established.   But how they are to be interpreted in their bearing on the nature of sense-*experience* is a question to which neither ordinary consciousness nor the positive sciences can give any satisfactory answer, and which on philosophical investigation has proved surprisingly difficult and proportionately contentious.

C

(ii.) DESCARTES' ALTERNATIVE

There is, however, one answer which has such initial plausibility that until it had been tried and found wanting, no other could at all hope to receive a hearing; and it was upon this misleading scent that Descartes and all his disciples hurried off in full cry. Only one conclusion can seemingly be drawn. The processes, physical and physiological, above enumerated, must have as their ultimate function the bringing into existence, or at least the occasioning so to exist, of certain entities, viz. those which we are now accustomed to entitle *sensations* of light and colour. These entities, Descartes further argues, differ in quite radical fashion from the antecedents which generate them. For whereas these antecedents are mechanical processes, occurring in public space, the resulting sensations are, he contends, not so describable, and occur in what may be entitled the field of consciousness. If, then, we picture the self, as Descartes virtually did, as standing over against the sensations and as apprehending them, the following diagram, in which the self, as befits a self-centred existence, is pictorially represented by a circle, will illustrate crudely, but not altogether incorrectly, the cognitive situation, as Descartes thus conceived it. In ordinary consciousness the self seems to itself to look out through the eye at X^1; what alone it directly experiences is X^2; and X^2 is a copy, image, or representation of X^1, constructed by the self, in the light of past experience, out of the sensations that X^1 arouses by acting on the eye, and through the eye, on the brain. X^1 is invisible. What alone can be seen is X^2; and it is not a material body, but a mental image in the field of consciousness.

It may be called a representation; it represents, as by deputy, the outer, independently existing material body.

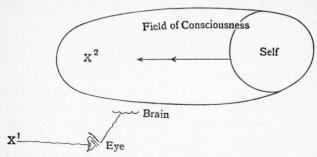

Thus if ten people, standing in a circle, look at an orange which one of the ten holds up to view, there will then exist eleven oranges—one separate orange in each of the ten separate fields of consciousness, and in addition the invisible orange which one of the ten is holding in his hand. Material bodies, by the mere fact of being external, are, on this view, necessarily invisible. Not only is the mind of each individual incapable of directly experiencing anything non-mental; it cannot transcend the field of its own private consciousness. Objects, in order to be apprehended, must be reduplicated in a private mental form, that is, as images; and these, it is alleged, are as dependent upon the individual's mind as reflections are upon the mirror in which they appear. We cannot see one another's bodies any more than we can see one another's minds. Nothing penetrates into any consciousness save in the shadowy form of a mental duplicate.

Descartes adopts a similar attitude in regard to the sense of touch. If I place my hand upon a desk, I seem to myself to have an immediate apprehension of the cool hard surface of the desk as it presses against the palm of my hand.   But here again scientific reflection would seem to show that in adopting this attitude we are subject to an illusion.   The surface of the hand is not itself any more sensitive than is the surface of the desk.   What happens is that the desk acts chemically on certain temperature - organs and mechanically upon certain pressure-organs in the inner skin of the hand.   In both cases nerve-vibrations are aroused, and the two types of vibrations pass severally to the sensory regions of temperature and of contact in the hemispheres.   In connection therewith there arise in the percipient's field of consciousness sensations of temperature and contact; and out of these sensations, using them as data, he constructs for himself, as best he can—with the aid of past experiences similarly aroused and now recalled—a mental picture or copy of the surface which is acting on the end-organs. Just as material bodies are invisible, so likewise they are intangible.

(iii.) GALILEO AND DESCARTES

This doctrine of representative perception was, in Descartes' own philosophy, supplemented by a doctrine of pure thought, according to which we have direct, purely conceptual, apprehension of the independently real.   But subject to this important qualification, with which, since we are at present dealing with *sense*-experience, we need not here concern ourselves,[1] the above statement of the doctrine emphasises what was mainly influential in determining Descartes' attitude to his metaphysical problems, and especially to the

---

[1] Cf. below, pp. 30-32.

problem of the relation of mind and body. He was, he believed, constrained to acceptance of the doctrine by the physical teaching of his younger contemporary, Galileo, and by the necessity, as he himself contended, of employing similar methods in the biological sciences. In Descartes' time philosophy and science were not distinguished from one another; and the doctrine of representative perception was therefore in his eyes as much the direct outcome of scientific inquiry as any of the more specific conclusions to which it had led.[1] As we shall find, much of the mischief which the doctrine has caused in philosophy, and its persistence in face of criticism, are due to this belief that no other interpretation of sense-experience is consistent with the teaching of the positive sciences, and that it alone, therefore, has the prestige of these sciences behind it.

This belief has indeed considerable seeming justi-fication. The distinction drawn by Galileo in his *Il Saggiatore* between the mechanical properties by which objects causally influence one another, and the other seemingly otiose [2] qualities by which they are sensu-

---

[1] In my *Studies in the Cartesian Philosophy* I have tried to show that the dualism between mind and matter, in which the doctrine of representative perception has its roots, is not to be understood in the manner in which Descartes has himself expounded it, namely, as being the final outcome of his philosophising. As involved in the general and scientific thought of his time, the dualism constituted his initial problem, and predetermined many of the conclusions at which he believed himself to have arrived by independent argument.

[2] The behaviour of billiard balls is not affected by their colours; a red ball acts on a green ball in the same manner in which it acts on a white one. That is to say, the colours play no part in the interactions: the effects are constant even when the colours vary. Only so is the game fair and square, as between the players. Though Galileo does not so express himself, his reason for holding that the mechanical properties of shape and motion have to be ascribed to bodies while the other qualities cannot be so ascribed, has its source in this difference between efficiency and non-efficiency, as I proceed to indicate, on pp. 23-5.

ously differentiated, led him at once to the conclusion that the secondary [1] qualities have "their residence exclusively in the sensitive [animated] body," and " would all be removed and annihilated were the animal removed."

Galileo does not here go the length of saying that the secondary qualities are mental, but he quite definitely holds that they have no existence in the strictly physical realm. The sole reason which he assigns for this view is the fact that they are not in thought bound up with the concept of physical existence; and this of course means that they are not among the properties which are required to account for the behaviour of material bodies. A feather, applied lightly to some part of the body, causes tickling. By general admission this does not justify us, Galileo points out, in ascribing the tickling to the feather, as an inherent quality. The feather can do no more than move and touch the skin. The tickling depends entirely upon us (*è tutta di noi*), and must cease with the removal of the animated and sensitive body. " I believe that many qualities which are attributed to natural bodies, tastes, odours, colours, and others have to be regarded as of similar, and not greater, existence." [2]

The character of physical explanation, as still usually conceived in the sixteenth and seventeenth

[1] Though the terms primary and secondary were first introduced by Locke, it is convenient to employ them in defining the distinction as drawn by Galileo. The primary qualities are usually described as being those qualities which are apprehended both by touch and by sight, viz. extension or spatial size, shape, and motion. The secondary qualities, similarly described, are those which are apprehended only by a single sense, as sweet and sour by taste, the odours by smell, heat and cold by the temperature senses, sound by hearing, and colour by sight. Difficulties arise in regard to the quality of ' solidity,' and its relation to motor sense.

[2] *Il Saggiatore*, § 48, *Opere* (1844), tomo iv. p. 334.

centuries, must have had considerable influence in determining Galileo's position. The Aristotelian physics, in opposition to which Galileo was formulating his own standpoint, had accepted qualitative change as *the* physical occurrence *par excellence*. Hot bodies become cold; white objects become black. Galileo, conceiving physical fire and physical colour as forms of matter and motion, was constrained to hold that if heat and colour in their various *qualitative* modes are physical existences, they are existences in regard to which the science of physics can have nothing to say. They do not need to be taken into account in explaining the behaviour and causal agency of material bodies; and accordingly if physical are otiose, or to use an equivalent technical term, epiphenomenal. For these reasons Galileo, without further or special argument, at once adopts the view that these qualitatively varying experiences are to be conceived on the analogy of the organic sensations and feelings, and therefore as falling outside the physical domain. If strictly physical, qualitative changes would, it would seem, have to be conceived as involving annihilation and creation, with the added difficulty that we should be unable to assign any causes for their production save the strictly physical, non-qualitative differences of motion, size, etc., with which they appear in correlation. That even on the view adopted they still (like tickling and the organic sensations generally) have to be conceived as being creatively brought into existence, is indeed true. But the causes which, on the new view, can be alleged as creatively producing them, involving, as they do, all the complex factors that go to make life and consciousness possible, are not so patently insufficient. And what is more immediately important, the task of accounting for their occurrence no longer falls to the physicist. He is released from all obligation in the matter, beyond showing that when the secondary 'qualities' are conceived as being in their physical nature modes of matter and motion, the stimuli supplied to the senses are such as will suffice, as physical 'occasions,' to start off the complex physiological processes upon which the *qualitative* differences, directly experienced, are now supposed to depend.

The next step was taken by Descartes. Generalising Galileo's physical principles, he treated them as being likewise applicable to biological occurrences and as capable of yielding an explanation no less exhaustive than that which they yield of events in the inorganic realm. But when physiological phenomena are viewed in this manner as a subspecies within the strictly physical, the secondary qualities have to be extruded from the entire material world, and have to be regarded as modifications of the only other type of existence which then remains, namely, the mental. And thus arose what Whitehead[1] has so felicitously entitled that fatal doctrine of 'bifurcation,' whereby Descartes distinguished between the psychical, conceived as comprehending all the secondary 'qualities' and physical entities conceived as endowed with merely mechanical properties.

It is not sufficient to say that these two realms are characterised by opposite types of predicates, and are therefore dualistically conceived. They constitute a contrast of the most amazing and incredible kind. Whereas within the physical domain creation and annihilation can never be found to occur, these are

---

[1] *The Concept of Nature,* pp. 30, 185, 187.

the most usual occurrences of the mental realm.
Creation, it is asserted, is the prerogative of finite no
less than infinite mind.   The secondary ' qualities '
are psychic additions which each finite mind is competent, when occasioned thereto by physical stimuli,
to add to the sum of the pre-existent.   And when
these ' qualities ' cease to be thus creatively supported
in existence by some one individual, they pass into
nothingness.   Even the ' memory ' of them, as Descartes held, is a chapter in physiology.   They do not
in passing leave mental vestigia of any kind.   In being
' recalled ' they have to be recreated upon the occasion
of brain-processes which follow the paths mechanically
formed by the original bodily processes.

When the aims of the positive sciences are thus
interpreted in strictly mechanical terms, all qualitative
changes are shouldered off into the mental realm.
The physicist is well satisfied to be thus able to expel
them from his territory; and when the physiologist,
following his example, does so likewise, they fall to
be treated by the psychologist.   And since there is no
further domain into which they can be ejected, the
psychologist has to come to terms with the many
puzzling problems which they involve, either by some
such type of epiphenomenalism as the physicist has
been so careful to avoid, or, upon the bankruptcy of
this way of thinking, by means of parallelism, or,
when this likewise proves untenable, by falling back
upon that biological restatement of nineteenth-century
epiphenomenalism which is now current under the
title behaviourism.

CHAPTER III

ARGUMENT IN SUPPORT OF THE DOCTRINE OF REPRESENTATIVE PERCEPTION

In addition to the immense boon which the doctrine of representative perception affords to the physicist and physiologist, in removing from their domains the seemingly insoluble problems involved in qualitative change, there are certain other advantages which are so obvious and, as it would seem, so little capable of being dispensed with, that the doctrine has, up till a few decades ago, met with almost universal acceptance among scientists and psychologists, and until Kant with well-nigh universal acceptance among specialists in philosophy.

(i.) THE ADVANTAGES OF THE DOCTRINE

What other theory, it may be said, can offer so simple and obvious an explanation of colour-blindness, of variations in our experience of heat according to the temperature of the skin, of the variations in sound, colour, size, etc., with distance, and indeed of the entire arrangement of the visual field according to perspective? If each individual is constrained to rely entirely upon his own private sensations for knowledge of the public world, are not those variations just such as we should expect to occur? The advance of psychology, so far from rendering the theory less easy of application, appears rather to enforce its cogency. Do not the explanations given by the psychologist of the many new types of illusion, which he has himself discovered, or to which at least he has drawn special attention (such as in the estimation of size by touch, according to the sensitiveness of the portions of the skin brought into action, and in the estimation of solidity by the eye in monocular and binocular vision), imply the essential truth of the doctrine?

Again, what other doctrine will suffice to account for the well-nigh complete differences which we find to exist between objects as sensuously apprehended and the actual nature of these objects as determined through scientific investigation? A drop of water appears to the eye to be a whitish-coloured piece of continuous matter, the parts of which are at rest. Yet, as the physicist informs us, when more correctly apprehended, it is found to consist of discrete molecules which are not at rest, and which, if coloured, can be coloured only in minute spots and not as wholes. For, as the physicist demonstrates, the term molecule —so far as shape and size are referred to—stands only for the space within which a certain number of atoms (in the case of a molecule of water, two of hydrogen and one of oxygen) confine their vibratory motions. As Lord Kelvin has calculated, these atoms are in size, relatively to the volume of the molecule, as three footballs would be to the space occupied by St. Paul's Cathedral; they occupy the molecule very much in the manner in which a small military force may occupy an extensive territory, not by bulk but by mobility. Even, therefore, if the molecules are at rest, their constituents are in constant motion; and if they be coloured, the colour can be located (so long at least as we keep to usual ways of thinking) only in the atoms, not in the ' empty,' and relatively vast, molecular spaces within which they lie.

But present-day science, revising the views which it held until recently, intervenes to interdict even these conclusions. The atom, as regards size and shape, is viewed not as solid and continuous, but as a name only for the space within which still smaller bodies move and interact. Each atom reduces without re-mainder to a set of spatially ordered electrons. To extend Lord Kelvin's calculation.[1] If the size of each atom be conceived as yet further magnified to the size of a parish church, the electrons composing it will then be about the size of full stops in ordinary print, each in constant motion within the limits of the church. The inadequacies of our original sense - perception are thus again demonstrated, in a still more striking manner.

There is, indeed, a quite definite sense in which the drop of water as a *whole* is at rest, relatively to its surroundings. So far our sense-perception yields correct knowledge. Similarly, if we insist upon taking a naïvely realistic view of colour, we can argue that the colour of the drop of water may, in some manner not yet definable, correlate with the drop as a whole. Just as there is a surface tension over the whole surface of the drop, generated by the proximity of the molecules to one another, so, it can be contended, there may be a state of tension over the entire surface

---

[1] Cf. Duncan, *The New Knowledge*, p. 151. Physical science is pro-gressing so rapidly that this further calculation, as made by Sir Oliver Lodge and Mr. Duncan, is already somewhat out of date. For our pur-poses it is, however, sufficiently in keeping with later results.

and throughout its transparent interior determining its whiteness. Or again we can argue, that if its multitudinous constituents be coloured, then even though they may not all possess the same colour, they may yet, owing to their constant and rapid movements, like a disk with variously coloured sections when set in rotation, 'appear' uniformly coloured to the eye. These latter positions would, however—other objections apart—be purely conjectural; no empirical evidence can be offered in their support. For since, as already pointed out,[1] colours are causally inefficacious, only direct acquaintance can yield knowledge of their actual existence. Their conditions, whether physical or physiological, cannot, by any indirectly obtainable evidence, be shown to be themselves coloured.

Thus the drop of water, as conceived by science, differs in almost every respect from the water as we see it. Its constituents, viewed as forming a single whole, can, indeed, be at rest relatively to their surroundings. Also, the drop as seen may indicate roughly in its outline the region within the limits of which these constituents exist, and from which they exercise influence upon outside bodies. But the water is *not* a single continuous piece of quiescent and uniformly coloured matter. It is a swarm of discrete particles, which are immensely far apart proportionately to their size, and which are in continuous motion. Nor as to its colour or lack of colour do we have any sufficient evidence; and if we may argue from general probabilities, should it possess colour, there is little likelihood that the colouring is uniform.

Upon the doctrine of representative perception there is no difficulty in accepting the revolutionary

[1] Cf. above, p. 21 ff.

views to which modern physics thus finds itself committed. If our sole data for apprehending in sense-perception the nature of bodies be those sensations which accompany processes elaborately mediated by the sense-organs and nervous system, disparity between objects as immediately apprehended and objects as scientifically determined is even more easy of acceptance than would be a proved agreement.[1] It is entirely a question of what the detailed evidence, discoverable only by processes of elaborate indirectness, may constrain us to conclude. In any case, already in the time of Galileo and Descartes the disparity was sufficiently obvious. That it is even greater than they had grounds for believing, makes no essential difference.

(ii.) OBJECTIONS MET BY A BIOLOGICAL RESTATEMENT OF THE DOCTRINE

(a) Descartes' Rationalism

One main difficulty which stood in the way of the doctrine of representative perception was that of harmonising its view of sense-experience as a form of *knowledge* with the illusory and deceptive character of the information which sense-perception yields. So impressed was Descartes by this feature of sense-experience that in addition to his ontological dualism between mind and matter he resorted to a second dualism, within the mind itself, between the sensuous and the conceptual. Concepts, he maintained—it is one of the many paradoxes which render his philosophy, while seemingly so straightforward, in actual character

---

[1] How, when the disparity is so great, science can be developed out of ordinary experience, is a question which we shall consider later.

quite strangely sophisticated—are, both in nature and in origin, independent of the sensuous embodiments in and through which we appear to acquire knowledge of them. Concepts, he declared, are innate in the mind; it is out of them, not out of our misleading sense-experiences, that science is developed. These concepts, so far as they bear on experience of the outer world, are few in number and simple in composition —concepts of space, number, and motion, or at most of the fundamental modes thereof, together with the concepts of substance and causality; and when attentively studied in pure thought, they suffice to deliver us from the illusions to which we are committed by sense-experience. Sensations, Descartes concludes, are in all cases obscure and confused feelings, to which the finite mind is delivered over owing to its present connection with the brain. The brain is not the organ of our thinking, though it is the organ of our sensuous feelings and memories. Thought functions quite independently of the brain,[1] unaccompanied by any correlative brain-processes; and just for this reason it is capable of revealing the absolute nature of the independently real.

Descartes accordingly condemns our *sense*-experience as concealing from us the true nature of reality, and as not being what we usually interpret it as being, a correct apprehension of the world we live in. We must free the mind from all entanglement with the senses; we must emancipate our thinking from the tyranny of the sensuous imagination; we must in pure,

---

[1] According to Descartes, this follows, among other reasons, from the distinction between universals and particulars. Concepts, being universals, cannot be caused by brain-processes all of which are necessarily particular. It is noteworthy that the adherents of present-day behaviourism strongly incline to nominalism.

independent thought develop the content of those ultimate concepts which, while they make true knowledge possible, and indeed even such little knowledge as sense-experience may yield, *have no connection with any of the experiences which gain entry through the avenues of sense*. It is Descartes' voice that is speaking when Locke, in despite of his professed advocacy of an empirical method, startles us by declaring that: "General certainty is never to be found but in our ideas. Whenever we go to seek it elsewhere in experiment or observations without us, our knowledge goes not beyond particulars. It is the contemplation of our own abstract ideas that alone is able to afford us general knowledge." [1] "[Did we know the real essence of gold,] it would be no more necessary that gold should exist, and that we should make experiments upon it, than it is necessary for the knowing the properties of a triangle, that a triangle should exist in any matter; the idea in our minds would serve for the one as well as the other." [2]

(b) Sense-perception not primarily a Form of Knowledge

What is true and what is false in this teaching first became clear when the biological sciences, adopting evolutionary hypotheses, prepared the way for a less exclusively intellectualist treatment of sense-perception. For when we approach sense-experience from the standpoint of biology, there is every reason for questioning the apparently obvious assertion that the function of sense-experience is to enable us to gain *knowledge* of the world around us. The function of

[1] *Essay* IV. vi. 16.   [2] *Essay* IV. vi. 11.   Cf. II. xxxii. 24; IV. xii. 12.

sense-perception, as of instinct, is not knowledge but power, not insight but adaptation; and accordingly the qualities and merits of our perceptions are only to be understood in the light of practical criteria which determine whether the perceptions are or are not suited to practical needs. Purely theoretical criteria are here no less inadequate and misleading, as grounds for eulogistic or depreciatory judgment, than they would be in any attempt to estimate the part played in an animal's life by this or that sense-organ.

For what is it that Nature has, so to speak, in view when it endows an animal with the capacity for sense-experience? That the animal may be equipped for avoiding its enemies, finding its food, and satisfying its various instinctive needs. For these purposes objects do not have to be known as they exist in themselves. Thus a dog, in order to recognise water and to be able to satisfy its thirst by lapping it with the tongue, does not need to apprehend its molecular, atomic, and sub-atomic structure. That would be a harmful complication. The animal would be bewildered by the multitudinous dancing particles; its limited amount of discriminative attention, required as it is for the apprehension of the stimuli that indicate food, danger, etc., would be exhausted long before it was well under way. The animal preoccupied with the unnecessary would be unable to survive to take advantage of the knowledge thus obtained.

(c) The Functions of the Secondary Qualities

In these considerations we find an at least partial explanation of the existence and employment of the

D

secondary qualities; and it is an explanation which appears to be entirely in harmony with the doctrine of representative perception. If the apprehension of material bodies in their actual independent nature and in all their complexity is incompatible with the purposes for which sense-perception is evolved, some other *definite* mode in which they may present themselves must be provided. A mere blurring of their outline, a simple ignoring of their constitution, will not suffice. The sense-perceptions must be definite, and for the purposes which they serve accurate and precise. This is especially obvious in regard to our human sense-perceptions. Upon them rest all our various dexterities and manual arts, as well as our delicate appreciations of subtle beauties in texture and design.

How, then, can simplification and alteration proceed without sacrifice of definiteness, that is, without incapacitating us from having a delicately discriminative apprehension of all those details which are necessary for the guidance of the more complex adaptive and manipulative movements? Nature has succeeded in meeting these seemingly conflicting requirements by the ingenious invention of the secondary qualities. The senses, it may be noted, function as telepathic organs. They enable us to apprehend what is happening either at a distance from the body or at a distance from the brain. Through the tastes we learn what is happening in the mouth, and so can decide as to what foods are or are not beneficial to the body. Through the thermal sensations we gain information as to the temperatures playing on the surface of the body, and so can guard ourselves against excessive cold and heat. Through sound we learn of movements, threatening or helpful, throughout the whole extent of a very wide environment, and are able to determine whether they are near or distant. But it is in sight that the admirable effectiveness of Nature's devices is most apparent. For through sight we apprehend the external world in a personal perspective which defines at a glance the spatial three-dimensional relations in which objects stand to the body, and in terms of diversity of colour and shading their motions, shapes, and relative sizes. All this is secured through those various illusions which constitute perspective— objects changing in shape, dwindling in size, being high or low in the field of vision, etc.—and by those still more deep-rooted illusions whereby objects appear to possess as an inherent property some specific colour or shade of light. These latter illusions are the means whereby Nature secures to us an apprehension of the outline of each object in distinction from the background against which it stands and from the differently coloured and shaded nearer objects that may overlap and partially conceal it. By the same means we are enabled to discriminate within each object the detail of its visible superficial parts.

Against the objection that these perceptions, when tested by a theoretical standard, are false and illusory, that objects do not have, or at least that we have no sufficient evidence that they have, any such colours, and that even the *apparent* [1] shapes and sizes of the objects are determined by standards of strictly practical convenience, Nature needs no defence. The problem which Nature has thus solved, that of enabling animals and man to maintain themselves successfully in a difficult environment, is a strictly practical problem;

[1] Cf. below, p. 115 ff.

and sense - perception as a practical device cannot legitimately be tested by standards of a theoretical or scientific character.

But if a defence, on these lines, be called for, it is at once forthcoming. Here, as so frequently elsewhere, Nature kills two very different birds with one and the same stone. Though sense-experience originates in order to meet strictly practical needs, its data have, as a matter of fact, likewise made possible man's acquisition of theoretical insight. The practical devices do, it is true, involve illusion; but they have served their purpose without closing the path that leads to genuine knowledge of the independently real. They may have rendered the path more indirect and circuitous than it might otherwise have had to be—if indeed any alternative to the path actually followed can be allowed as possible. Human ingenuity, however, though at times hard pressed to escape from sensory perspectives and to penetrate behind them to their generating causes, has not yet come upon any insuperable obstacle preventive of further advance. And Nature might also plead that her device of the secondary qualities, besides making both ordinary and scientific experience possible, has justified itself in and through the fine arts. For there also the secondary qualities have shown their fitness to subserve values of a higher order than the strictly practical. Besides conditioning survival, they are the means indispensable to still other goods.[1]

Thus the secondary qualities can no longer be viewed in the manner of Descartes, Spinoza, and Leibniz, as *obscure* and *confused* apprehensions of

[1] Cf. below, p. 229 ff.

realities which they conceal from our view. They exist in their own right, and they vindicate their reality, as do the primary qualities, by the indispensable part which they play in Nature's ordered and complex economy. In their absence animal and human senses could not supply data for a sufficiently rapid apprehension, in a manner at once comprehensive in extent and discriminating as regards detail, of everything that is essential for the purposes of adaptation. Nor in their absence could, at a later stage, either science or the fine arts have become possible.

The comparison of the secondary qualities to the organic sensations, such as (to take Galileo's instance) tickling, may be more or less adequate if we have in mind only those qualities which are yielded by the lower senses. But even in this reference the analogy is biassed by Galileo's intention to view them as being, in contrast to the primary qualities, unreal and subjective. Such a view is more plausible as regards tastes than as regards odours, temperatures, and sounds; and it is entirely inadequate when applied to light and colour. Colour is a genuinely objective entity, and like temperature is one of the main clues by study of which the scientist penetrates ever deeper into the secrets of Nature.[1] The division of reality into the merely mechanical and the purely mental fails to do justice to the diverse levels upon which Nature works; and recognition of this fact is one of the main features through which present-day statements of the doctrine of representative perception differ from the account given by Descartes. Supporters of the doctrine continue, however, to regard our knowledge

---

[1] Cf. the use of spectra in astronomy and of methods of staining in the biological sciences.

of external reality as being mediate—a position which, I should contend, is due to their failure to take account of the diverse factors which co-operate in knowledge. These, however, are aspects of the situation to which I shall return.[1]

---

[1] Cf. below, pp. 49, 74-6, 178 ff., 229 ff.

CHAPTER IV

ARGUMENT IN CRITICISM OF THE DOCTRINE OF REPRESENTATIVE PERCEPTION

I SHALL now proceed to consider some of the main objections to which the doctrine of representative perception would seem to lie open. These objections are certainly not less cogent than the arguments by which the doctrine is upheld; and when we have reviewed them, we shall be in a position to appreciate the very strange quandary in which philosophy has unhappily found itself.

(i.) PHILOSOPHY'S PRESENT QUANDARY

On the one hand, we have the subjectivist teaching of Berkeley and of those who follow in his train. Though Berkeley adopts Locke's view that sensa are not, as Descartes had maintained, modes of mind, but are its objects, he none the less cuts away from the doctrine of representative perception all its more genuinely realist implications. There is, he contends, no independently existing material world; the teaching of the natural sciences, when properly interpreted, demands no such assumption; Nature consists in the sensa, and therefore must ultimately be accounted for exclusively in terms of them. So forcible and convincing is Berkeley's teaching in this regard, that even to this day many leading scientific thinkers agree in contending that only from a subjectivist standpoint can either the ultimate purposes or the present results of the positive sciences be correctly viewed.   This is, for instance, the standpoint of Karl Pearson and of Ernst Mach—the latter of whom stands for the sole type of philosophy which has, it would seem, exercised any considerable influence upon Einstein.   On the other hand, we have a few philosophers, such as Reid and Kant, challenging this teaching, but gaining a hearing mainly among specialists in philosophy, and, as we find upon examining their teaching, being much more definite in criticism than in construction.   Their efforts to provide an alternative view are, indeed, far from successful, and seem to disclose the continuing influence in their own thinking of those very principles from which they profess to have broken away.   Also, whatever be the merits of the counter-doctrines which they propose, these have never been so formulated as to be understandable by non-professional students of metaphysics.   Accordingly it has inevitably followed that the main trend of influence, at least as regards popular and scientific thought, has been on the lines of the Cartesian teaching.   It has been modified, partly under Berkeleian and partly under sceptical and naturalistic influences, and it has, as we have seen, been restated in the light of biological data; but, however thus altered or amplified, that which renders it essentially subjectivist has continued to exercise a predominant influence.   Even in the philosophical disciplines this is what has happened— at least frequently so in ethics, and almost invariably so in psychology.   Whether the many assaults now being made upon the subjectivist position are to be more successful, or whether they are, at best, to be incidental victories in a campaign which as a whole is to result in defeat, remains to be seen.

(ii.) The Alternation between Realism and Subjectivism

The first and main criticism which has to be passed upon the doctrine of representative perception is that the argument in its support starts from a realist stand-point inconsistent with the conclusions to which the doctrine itself commits us. It is only by assuming that we are acquainted with real objects that the subjectivist obtains his starting-point, namely, real material bodies acting on the material brain, and through the brain generating or occasioning ideas in the mind. The external objects are separated from their effects, the ideas, by a large number of inter-mediate processes, physical and physiological, to which they bear no resemblance, save in being spatially con-ditioned. Even granting, therefore, that ideas can legitimately be regarded as effects of the brain-states thus caused, the facts which prove that ideas are effects due to intermediate processes set agoing by outside objects justify no assertion as to their resemblance to these objects, and so must undermine the realist assumption with which the argument starts. There can, it would seem, be no ground save only the *deus ex machina* of a pre-established harmony for retaining our primitive belief that they are qualified to reveal material bodies.

Thus the realist view of ideas, as yielding know-ledge of external objects, must be accepted as valid if the subjectivist argument is to have a starting-point;

it is little likely to be valid if the subjectivist argument be correct. Either, therefore, the subjectivist must establish his position without assuming the ultimate truth of his starting-point, or he must recognise the truth of this starting-point as casting doubt upon the conclusion reached.

This argument has in one form or another been so frequently stated, and in spite of its simplicity seems to be so cogently valid, that as a rule subjective idealists now recognise its force. They therefore endeavour to start from facts which involve no realist assumptions. And, in so doing, they generally propound their argument in the form of an argument from relativity. Even while remaining within the field of ordinary consciousness, our perceptions can, they contend, be proved to be subjective, numerically and existentially distinct in the mind of each observer.

(iii.) THE ARGUMENT FROM RELATIVITY IN ITS PHYSIOLOGICAL FORM

Let us first consider this argument from relativity in the form in which it is most naturally first propounded, namely, in connection with the physiological concomitants of our mental experiences. We can then proceed to consider the non-physiological restatement of it. Sense-perceptions are, as is easily shown, conditioned by the individual circumstances, viewpoint, and previous experience of each observer. They vary concurrently with changes in the relation of our bodies to the objects, as when objects alter in apparent size and form according to their distance from us. Or they may vary in correspondence with variations within our bodies, as when what is red to

the ordinary observer is grey to the colour-blind, or
as when objects are seen double upon displacement
of one eyeball.   Thus the exact nature of the variations can only be accounted for in and through determination of all the various influences which are acting
on the brain.   The perceptions vary independently of
the objects apprehended, and directly only with the
brain-states.   They are conditioned, mediately by
objects, immediately by the brain-states which are
dependent on bodily conditions as well as on external
stimuli.

These, then, are the ' facts '; they can neither be
called in question nor ignored; they constitute the
problem which awaits solution.   How are they interpreted by the subjectivist?   He may argue in either
of two ways.   If he believes that our mental states
carry us to a trans-subjective world, material in character, he will argue from this conditionedness of our
perceptions to their subjectivity.   He will contend
that since our perceptions vary directly only with the
brain-states, they must be effects distinct from the
real objects and separately existent in each individual
mind.   But, obviously, in so arguing the subjectivist
falls back upon the realist interpretation of experience.
The argument from relativity, when stated in this
manner, reduces to the previous argument from causal
dependence of experience upon the brain.

(iv.) The Argument from Relativity in its Non-physiological Forms

The subjectivist may, however, take a very different
line, and so may seek to evade the force of the above
objections.   He may entirely give up the belief in an

independent, material world, and consequently in the existence of a material body and brain. He may contend that the only possible objects of the mind are sensations; and from this position he may then argue that the objects thus immediately known are subjective for a twofold reason: first, because they are sensations; and secondly, because they are relative to each observer, varying from mind to mind.

(a) Failure to distinguish between Sensing and Sensa

To take these two arguments in order: even without questioning that the objects known are sensations, we may dispute the inference that they are therefore subjective. Thanks to Ward, Moore, Stout, and others, it is now very generally recognised that ' sensation ' is an ambiguous term. It is used with two very different meanings, as process of apprehension and as object apprehended. If sensation is mental process, then for this sufficient reason it must fall on the subjective side. But if, on the other hand, sensations have to be regarded not as mental processes, but as objects revealed in and through such processes, this argument will fall to the ground. Though red is known only as sensation, it is undoubtedly an objective content. It is not a state of the subject, but an object to the subject. Similarly, a sound or an odour or a taste is an object apprehended by the mind, and is therefore distinct from the processes in which such apprehension consists. Nothing but confusion can result from employing the term ' sensation ' in both these conflicting connotations. The ambiguity is very similar to that which makes the term ' experience,' which may mean either experiencing or the experienced, so serviceable to certain contemporary schools of philosophy. It may be said that the two aspects—process of apprehension and object apprehended—are inseparable; but even granting this, they are none the less distinguishable. A name which is adequately descriptive of the one aspect cannot rightly be applied to the other.

The subjectivist argument, that objects as known are sensations, and therefore are subjective, makes use of this fundamental ambiguity. Only by interpreting sensations as signifying objective contents can it justify the assertion that objects as known are sensations; and yet only by regarding sensations as mental processes can it legitimate the inference that they are therefore subjective. The ground of the argument involves one interpretation of the term ' sensation,' the conclusion implies the other. It is open to us to propound the counter-argument. Since sensations are only known as objects they are distinct from mental processes, and cannot be mental or subjective. This is the meaning now ascribed to the term ' sensation ' by such psychologists as Ward, Stout, and Binet. They limit it to denote objective content. Binet admits that there is no contradiction in speaking of an object both as sensation and as material.[1] He also

[1] Alfred Binet, *L'Âme et le corps* (1905), pp. 13, 63 ; Mr. Moore, in his " Refutation of Idealism," which appeared in *Mind* in 1903 (reissued in *Philosophical Studies*, 1922), preferred to employ ' sensation ' as signifying awareness. But while so doing, he expounded the position above adopted in the following very explicit terms: " The awareness which I have maintained to be included in sensation is the very same unique fact which constitutes every kind of knowledge : ' blue ' is as much an object and as little a mere content of my experience, when I experience it, as the most exalted and independent real thing of which I am ever aware. There is, therefore, no question of how we are to ' get outside the circle of our own ideas and sensations.' Merely to have a sensation is already to *be* outside that circle. It is to know something which is as truly and really *not* a part of *my* experience, as anything which I can ever know " (*Philosophical Studies*, p. 27).

points out that there is no reason why sensations, so regarded, may not have permanent existence. That is to say, the use of the term ' sensation,' when thus clearly defined, decides nothing either for or against realism.

Though Locke defines ' idea ' as signifying an object—" whatsoever is the object of the understanding when a man thinks " [1]—the other meaning of the term, viz. as an act of apprehension, as meaning ' idea of,' intervenes to determine his interpretation of all ideas as necessarily mind-dependent.[2]   And the latter sense—the history and etymological meaning of the term notwithstanding—is now, probably, its proper and most usual sense. Ideas are acts or processes of apprehension. We are conscious *in* and *through* them, not *of* them. They do not terminate thought, but enable the mind to transcend itself, and to apprehend things which are not ideas, not states of the mind. This, indeed, is what Locke himself teaches in other passages, though more by implication than in clearly thought-out terms, and in a manner which still preserves to ideas their mediating function,

[1] *Essay* I. i. 8.
[2] Cf. Gibson, *Locke's Theory of Knowledge and its Historical Relations*, pp. 19-21. " The idea for [Locke] is at once the apprehension of a content and the content apprehended; it is both a psychical existent and a logical meaning." " It is with ideas as ' objects ' of thought that the *Essay* is primarily concerned. The term ' object,' however, implies for Locke relation to and dependence upon a mind or subject. Thus while, as we have seen, he assumes throughout a realm of real being, independent of the cognitive process, but to which our knowledge ultimately refers, the constituents of this realm are not ' objects ' in his sense of the term, even at the moment in which they are thought of. Like Arnauld, again, he repudiates the supposition that ideas possess an existence apart from the act of thought by which their content is apprehended. ' Having ideas and perception,' he declares, are ' the same thing.' He is one ' who thinks ideas are nothing but perceptions of the mind.' "

as intervening between the mind and independently existing things.[1]

That Berkeley, though no less emphatic than Locke that ideas are ' *objects* of human knowledge,'[2] and as such opposite in nature to the mind which apprehends them, is yet in some degree influenced by these two meanings of the term ' idea,' seems at times to be shown by his use of the ambiguous phrase ' in the mind.' The only definite meaning of this phrase is inseparable from the mind, what is made possible through the mind; and that is only true of ideas as acts or processes; at least the contrary demands separate proof.

Berkeley's further argument, *that an idea can resemble nothing but an idea*, is invalid, if ' idea' be taken in this latter meaning. An act of apprehension need not resemble that of which it is the apprehension; they may differ to almost any extent. My idea of the North Pole is not to the north of my idea of the South Pole; the North Pole is extremely cold, but I can entertain it in idea without lowering the temperature even of the warmest of rooms. My apprehension of a red book is not itself red or heavy or hard, though it enables me to have ideas *of* these and the other qualities of the book.

But even allowing what Berkeley so explicitly

---

[1] Cf. Gibson, *op. cit.* p. 20: " It is, indeed, a fundamental misunderstanding of his position to suppose that, in his account of the genesis of our ideas, Locke sought to derive the whole content of our knowledge from a series of psychical facts devoid of objective reference. The function of the idea is repeatedly compared by him with that of the word. Both were for him essentially representative; and he would no more have thought of forming a theory of ideas which should treat them apart from their objective reference than he would have regarded as satisfactory an account of words which disregarded their possession of meaning."

[2] *Principles of Human Knowledge*, § 1.

asserts, that ideas are to be understood as objects
and not as acts of apprehension, the above principle,
that an idea can resemble nothing but an idea, will yet
not hold. We might as well argue that a reflection
cannot resemble anything but a reflection. A reflection differs fundamentally in its mode of existence
from that which is reflected. The real objects can
be touched; their reflections cannot. When we try
to touch them we touch only the mirror. The objects
have weight; the reflections have no weight. The
objects have permanent and independent existence—
at least special argument is required to prove the
contrary; the reflections are dependent on the mirror
and can only exist through it. And yet the reflections
do resemble their objects.

(b) Illegitimate Assumption that Sense-Perception must be Identical with Absolute Knowledge

But to return to our main theme, criticism of the
argument from relativity in its non-physiological forms:
we have still to consider that second form in which
the argument is propounded, namely, that since
sensations vary from mind to mind they must be
numerically and existentially distinct for each observer.
If by sensation were meant mental process, there
would be no question. Mental processes are admittedly subjective; they take place separately in the
mind of each conscious being. But since by ' sensation ' is meant content apprehended, *i.e.* a sensum,
the conclusion does not follow. The same identical
objective entity may, for all the argument itself shows
to the contrary, be apprehended by different minds,
and yet none the less be apprehended differently
by each mind. The subjectivist is making the

assumption that if we apprehend real objects in sense-experience, we must apprehend them in their intrinsic, absolute nature, and that, on a realist theory, as on his own theory, sense-perception must therefore be identical with scientific knowledge.[1]

A realist philosophy need not, however, proceed on any such assumption. Since Berkeley believes that objects exist only as ideas, and therefore only as known, he is entirely justified in holding to it; but it cannot, without further proof, be extended to objects regarded as causally efficacious and as existentially independent. The assumption is natural to subjectivism of the extreme type, but is not accepted (immediately at least) by realism. None the less, this is not the fundamental difference between the two theories ; it is rather that the subjectivist seeks to co-ordinate the varying sensations in terms of themselves, the realist by equating them with variations in the totality of the complex conditions, both subjective and trans-subjective, which he recognises to be involved. Or to state the same point in another way; the difference in attitude is that while the realist treats the sensed as being a function of several factors, the subjectivist treats the sensed as it stands, without reference to diverse factors at all.

[1] Cf. Mr. G. Dawes Hicks, *Proc. Arist. Soc.*, 1913–14, p. 42: "The reasoning would only be valid on the assumption that if the table is really coloured, the real colour *must* appear the same in darkness and in daylight, through a pair of blue spectacles and without them, in artificial light and in the sun's light—an assumption which, on the view I am taking, is at once to be dismissed as untenable. If the colour did appear to be the same in these varying circumstances, then certainly there would be reason, and sufficient reason, for doubting the reliability of visual apprehension. For obviously the conditions mentioned—real, objective conditions, as I take them to be—cannot be without influence upon any real colour the table may be said to possess."

E

The occurrence, therefore, of such variations as those above cited, is by itself no conclusive proof either for or against any one theory of knowledge. The variations constitute a problem to which different types of subjectivism and various forms of realism offer as many different solutions. The argument from relativity must be rejected as invalid. By itself it proves nothing, and would never have been put forward had not the subjectivist been already convinced on other grounds that the immediate objects of mind are strictly private. These other unexpressed grounds would seem ultimately to reduce to the physiological argument which I have already considered.

(v.) The Argument from Immediate Experience

Mr. Ward and Mr. Stout have, however, in recent times propounded yet another argument. They contend that, apart from all physiological considerations, the distinction between sensa and independent objects is directly evident *in immediate experience*. Thus Mr. Ward maintains that while we have immediate experience of ' extensity,' we have no experience of public space; and in proof of this contention he cites the fixity in size of the visual field, as immediately sensed.

" Whether, on shipboard, we look down at the deck, or away to the horizon, or upwards at the sky above us, the extensity of the colour sensation is in each case the same; the difference in the space seen is due to acquired perceptions involving movement." [1]

But is not Mr. Ward ignoring the third dimension, that of depth? This third dimension may be pro-

[1] *Naturalism and Agnosticism* (1899), vol. ii. p. 136.

gressively differentiated through our experiences of
motion, but our apprehension of it cannot be created
thereby.[1]   And when it is taken into account, it surely
rules out as illegitimate the supposition that all magnitudes, as immediately sensed, are projections upon
a single two-dimensional field, unvarying in size.
Extensity being always three-dimensional, we have no
right to assert that the landscape seen through a
window must be sensed as smaller than the frame of
the window.   Speaking for myself, I fail to discover
in my own sense-experience the existence of any such
flat field.   Definite discrimination of depths is certainly
a matter of acquired experience; but surely the same
is also true of lengths and sizes.   Mr. Ward's argument, if consistently pursued, must carry us back,
behind even the two-dimensional extensity, to the ' big,
blooming, buzzing confusion ' in which, as William
James contends, the world of the newly-born child
may be believed to consist.   If discrimination can
progressively disclose the two-dimensional relations
which are at first confusedly apprehended, it may also
be conceived as having progressively articulated the
three-dimensional world of developed consciousness.
Mr. Ward's argument rests on the contention that
sensa have a fixed, entirely intractable character, upon
which interpretation can exercise no transforming
influence.   So far as the ' secondary qualities ' in
abstraction from their spatial aspects are concerned,
this assumption would seem to be in accordance with
the facts.   But if we are justified in distinguishing
between sensing and intuiting, then, as we shall have
occasion to note,[2] there is a certain amount of empirical

---

[1] Cf. Broad, *Scientific Thought*, p. 290 ff.
[2] See below, pp. 76-9, and p. 114 ff.

evidence, not easily interpretable save as supporting the view that distance, size, and the like (*i.e.* those features which relate to the ' primary ' qualities) vary *sensuously* under varying conditions. As I shall also endeavour to show, these variations do not conflict with the belief that it is the actual independent objects which are being directly apprehended. Immediate experience, so far as my own introspective efforts enable me to judge, affords no evidence, either in the case of extensity or of any other sensory factor, that the experienced is ever an intermediary between the mind and its public world.

(vi.) The Determining Source of Subjectivism

Thus, so far as I can discover, subjective idealism has its source, exclusively, in a supposedly necessary deduction from the belief that sensations are mechanic-ally generated through brain-processes. Other argu-ments may be employed to develop the position, but they cannot be regarded either as originating or as justifying it.[1] The subjectivist, even when he seeks to ground his position exclusively on facts of relativity or of immediate experience, is still chiefly influenced by the physiological standpoint which he professes to reject.

Accordingly it does not matter from which side the subjectivist may approach the facts. He may start with the physicist and physiologist from material bodies and the material brain, or with the psychologist from our immediate mental experiences; in either case he lands himself in the same quandary. He can only

---

[1] On Berkeley's argument from the fact that increase of temperature ends in pain, cf. Broad, *Perception, Physics and Reality*, pp. 70-71,

prove things perceived to be subjective by proving
them to be externally related to objects as their
mechanical effects, and yet this can only be done by
simultaneously interpreting the things perceived in
a manner which the realist standpoint can alone justify.
This perpetual alternation between realism and idealism
is as contradictory as it is unavoidable.

Mr. Broad, while himself advocating a modified
form of representationism, frankly admits the force of
this objection:

" The belief that our sensa are appearances of something
more permanent and complex than themselves seems to be
primitive, and to arise inevitably in us with the sensing of the
sensa.   It is not reached by inference, and could not logically
be justified by inference.   On the other hand, there is no
possibility of either refuting it logically, or of getting rid of it,
or—so far as I can see—of co-ordinating the facts without it." [1]

Otherwise stated, the situation would seem to be
this: the subjectivist either tries to prove that what is
in his own mind is not in another person's mind by
showing that what is in the other person's mind under
certain circumstances is not in his own mind under
these circumstances, but in so doing assumes these
circumstances in a realist manner; or else he simply
asserts that what is in his own mind is not in the other
person's mind, and so lands in scepticism.   This
would seem to be what is meant by Hume in the
following passages:

" Do you follow the instincts and propensities of nature . . .
in assenting to the veracity of sense?   But these lead you to
believe that the very perception or sensible image is the external
object.   Do you disclaim this principle, in order to embrace a
more rational opinion, that the perceptions are only representa-

[1] *Scientific Thought*, p. 268.

tions of something external? You here depart from your internal propensities and more obvious sentiments; and yet are not able to satisfy your reason, which can never find any convincing argument from experience to prove that the perceptions are connected with any external objects." [1]

"That all [Berkeley's] arguments, though otherwise intended, are, in reality, merely sceptical, appears from this, *that they admit of no answer and produce no conviction.* Their only effect is to cause that momentary amazement and irresolution and confusion, which is the result of scepticism." [2]

(vii.) BERKELEY'S PERVERSE PROCEDURE

Berkeley's type of subjectivism is in this respect even more perverse than that of Descartes or Locke. For while Berkeley is more consistent in the working out of his conclusions, he just thereby proportionately weakens the foundations upon which his entire system rests. What he does is to accept the position adopted by his predecessors, namely, that all the mind can directly apprehend is ideas, and then to proceed to throw down the ladder by which alone it is possible to climb into this position. The evidence upon which Descartes bases his contention that material bodies are invisible and intangible is the evidence supplied by physics and physiology realistically interpreted. What Berkeley does is to deny the validity of this evidence, and yet none the less to hold to the results obtained by its means.[3]

---

[1] *An Enquiry Concerning the Human Understanding*, section xii. pt. i., towards the end.

[2] *Loc. cit. note.* Italics in text.

[3] Cf. Alexander, *Space, Time and Deity*, vol. i. p. 16 : " Berkeley saw the truth that there is no idea to act as middleman between the mind and external things, no veil betwixt the mind and reality. He found the reality therefore in the ideas themselves. The other alternative is not to discard the supposed world of reality behind the ideas but to discard the ideas,

Conceive an analogous situation. Let us, in the manner of Plato's allegory of the Cave, make the fanciful supposition that a person has all his life-long had his vision closed in by a mirror, that he has never seen anything save in this mirror, and that he has never been permitted to turn round and see the bodies which are being reflected. If some one, not subject to these limitations, were then to explain to him the nature of mirrors and of light and of the bodies which reflect the light, he would for the first time come to comprehend that what he sees in the mirror is not really there, and that the objects which he has hitherto believed to be real objects are, as his friend tells him, merely images which as such are only possible in a mirror, and which are therefore mirror-dependent.

But suppose, now, that he were a person with the ingenious mind of Berkeley. Might he not argue in reply that it is his friend who is deluded? " You are quite correct," he would say, " in maintaining that the objects which I apprehend are merely reflections, and can exist only in a mirror. But as to those bodies which you speak of as existing outside mirrors and as producing duplicates of themselves in mirrors, I have never myself seen any such objects, and I do not recognise the need of assuming them. The mirror itself, of which we speak, is the infinite, and therefore frameless, eternal Being that we name God. Moreover," he would proceed, " I am confirmed by what you say about light. You speak of light as an in-

---

regarded as objects dependent on the mind. . . . When the prejudice is removed that an object, because it owes its existence as an object to a subject, owes to that subject its qualities of white or green and its existence; the appeal lies from Berkeley to experience itself. So appealed to, my experience declares the distinct existence of the object as something non-mental."

visible something which can never be seen and has no colour. What are you saying except that light is not light, that colour is not really colour but only a vibration in a suspiciously strange kind of substance which you are pleased to call ether, and which like your alleged material substances can apparently exist where I have never seen anything to exist, outside the universal mirror. No," he would conclude, " what you tell me is too preposterously incredible. Objects can have only a mirror-like existence; the supposedly independent objects are *reflections*, and only exist as such."

Obviously this is to give away the whole case. In thus agreeing with his friend that the objects seen are reflections, he has committed himself to the view that they represent objects more real than themselves, and that it is by the intermediate agency of light-waves that they make their appearance. To deny the existence of such agencies while still regarding the reflections as reflections, is impossible. Yet this is what Berkeley virtually does when he agrees with Descartes and Locke that the objects immediately known are *ideas*. Just as when we speak of reflections as reflections we imply the existence of a mirror and of self-subsisting material bodies, so when Berkeley says that the objects known are ideas, he is ascribing to them a type of existence which can gain meaning only by contrast with another type which he yet asserts to be meaningless and inconceivable. He is questioning the physical and physiological evidence for Descartes' doctrine of representative perception, and yet is accepting the all-important conclusion to which the doctrine leads. That doctrine in its Cartesian form may not be, and as I believe is not, a valid doctrine; it can be questioned. But if so, it ought to be questioned as a whole. Its conclusions ought to be examined at least as rigorously as the premisses which have led to their adoption. If there be real material bodies acting directly, or through a medium, upon material sense-organs and the material brain, and if what we then directly experience comes into being as a result of the brain-processes thus caused, it may well be that the only possible, immediate, sensuous objects of mind are ideas, *i.e.* mind-dependent. But if such physiological arguments be invalid, are we not free to retain the commonsense view that objects are known directly face to face, that they are causally efficacious in their action upon one another, and have independent existence ? We are back in the realm of ordinary consciousness, and there is no longer any ground for questioning that different percipients apprehend one and the same independent, public world. As above argued, none of the special arguments by which Berkeley seeks to make good the elimination of Descartes' physical and physiological evidence seems able to survive a critical scrutiny.

This criticism can be restated in yet another way, suggested by Avenarius. The spatial world which we experience varies together with one particular part of itself, namely, with the brain. And this relation appears to be mutual; change in either involves change in both; they stand in functional relation, varying simultaneously with one another. This is the relation in which, according to physiology, the world, as *directly experienced*, is related to the brain. On the other hand, however, as the natural sciences likewise teach, objects are causally related to the brain and by their changes produce changes in it. This causal

relation, as involving sequence and implying independent, self-centred existence, holds only in the forward order, and therefore excludes the possibility of
simultaneous variation.   Which of the two attitudes
are we to adopt?[1]   Descartes, following in the steps
of physics and physiology, would have us accept both;
and so would commit us to the view that the world
directly experienced is not the real world, but only a
mental copy, private to each separate percipient.

Berkeley would have us accept only the latter part
of Descartes' conclusion, and yet rules himself out
from having the only kind of justification which
Descartes and the sciences have offered therefor.
There is, Berkeley teaches, no material brain existing
apart from experience and conditioning it.   Nothing
can exist save minds and the worlds which they immediately experience.   And so we are left with the
question to which Berkeley can give no sufficient
answer, how, if this be so, we need reject the realist
assumption of ordinary consciousness, that different
minds can directly experience the *same* objects and can
experience them as being, like the self, *independent,
causally efficacious* existences.

(viii.) FURTHER CRITICISM OF THE SUBJECTIVIST POSITION

There is yet another type of criticism to which the
doctrine of representative perception lies open, namely,

---

[1] I have considered Avenarius' views at greater length in two articles
entitled "Avenarius' Philosophy of Pure Experience" in *Mind*, N.S. vol. xv.
(1905), p. 13 ff.   "The fundamental problem of metaphysics is to reconcile
these two standpoints—the attitude of pure experience with the standpoint
adopted in physics and physiology.   How can the whole vary simultaneously with a part of itself, and with a part which is causally dependent
for its changes upon its relations to the rest of that whole?"

that it fails to deal with the problem which it sets out to explain, how knowledge is possible. When it has said its say, and has concluded that in all cases the objects apprehended are mental, not material, it proceeds, exactly in the manner of ordinary consciousness, to recognise as ultimate fact that these objects are *known*. No attempt is made to determine the nature of the knowing processes; the inquiry is solely as to the nature of the immediate objects which these processes disclose.[1]

Further the thesis, that the objects known are in all cases mental, while, as I shall try to show, not really rendering our capacity of knowing any the more intelligible, has had the unhappy effect of obscuring the essential nature of the self-transcendence which makes possible conscious experience. I have argued[2] that since bodies act upon and influence one another, self-transcendence may be regarded as characterising all existences. But this is no sufficient reason for ignoring the fact that in the conscious being we have a *type* and *degree* of self-transcendence which can only be misrepresented if interpreted on the analogy of causal affection, as ordinarily understood, namely, as being a process wherein a self-centred existence responds to external influence by a change wholly internal to itself.

This, however, is precisely what is done in subjectivist teaching. The mysterious power by which, in knowing, the self reaches out to other existences does not, it is argued, involve any transcendence of the limits inexorably imposed upon each finite being. It does not, for instance, demand any overcoming of the differences of spatial location. It consists solely

---

[1] Cf. below, p. 61.   [2] Cf. above, pp. 6-7.

in the self's capacity of self-knowledge. As embodied existences, we are so caught up into the unitary system of the material Universe that even the most distant objects are capable of modifying the self; and it is the modifications, thus caused, which alone are known. Each self *in potentia* is regarded as mirroring or rather reduplicating the entire Universe. The variety of Nature is brought within the mind; and the self being thus enlarged, self-knowledge is, it is claimed, adequate to the tasks imposed upon it.

We need not be surprised that this perverse method of resolving the paradoxes of knowledge should result in the contradictions above noted.[1] Its defects are but slightly concealed by the vagueness and ambiguity of the terms employed. Thus while at the start ' mind ' is taken as simply another name for the ' self,' and therefore as sharing in its supposed unity— is not the unity of the mind with itself the ground of its alleged capacity of self-knowledge?—none the less, in the course of the argument, the mind turns out to be distinct from the self, and to be a name for the field [2] that includes all those multitudinous states which are occasioned according as this or that object, near or distant, is acting upon the senses. And these states, even as occurring ' in the mind,' have to be recognised as possessing all the various properties through which natural existences differ from one another and from the self. Some, for instance, have spatial extension, and thereby stand in as marked contrast to the processes through which they are

[1] Cf. above, p. 41 ff.

[2] There is a similar vagueness in the bastard-phrase—at least it is so in a subjectivist context—'field of consciousness,' supposed to exist within the mind. The term ' field ' throws us back on spatial metaphor, not easily compatible with subjectivist teaching.

apprehended as do objects in actual space. But if so, why should we call in question the possibility of the outward looking attitude of ordinary consciousness? Why, if the self cannot recognise what lies outside itself, should we expect to find our apprehension of these objects any the more understandable when they are thus brought within the ' mind ' in the form of images? Are we not simply restating in a *subjectivist* form that fundamental fact of *self*-transcendence which in its initial, actually experienced, *realist* form, we have treated as paradox, and as such refused to recognise?

I have said [1] that subjectivism directs its efforts exclusively to determining the nature of the objects which consciousness discloses, and makes no attempt to determine the nature of conscious awareness itself. When it has concluded that the objects known are in all cases subjective or mental, or alternately, on the view of Locke and Berkeley, that they can be entitled ideas, it takes it as self-evident that the mind, whose states or ideas they are, should apprehend them. It argues that since awareness has been shown to be the apprehension by the self of its own states or ideas, all the explanation which any one, knowing when and where to stop, can reasonably demand has been given. And may it not be said that in accepting self-transcendence as an ultimate fact involved in all knowledge, I have as good as admitted this? The point here raised is important, and indeed quite fundamental in the theory of knowledge; and I must therefore endeavour, though at the expense of some little repetition, to remove the misunderstanding to which, as it seems to me, this objection is due.

First of all, as has frequently been pointed out, it

[1] Cf. above, p. 59.

should be clear that on *any* theory the possibility of direct, or immediate, knowledge must be taken as granted. What has *primarily* to be investigated is just this direct form of knowledge. The trustworthiness of indirect knowledge, inferential or other, must in all cases depend upon the trustworthiness of the direct processes through which its data are acquired. Since admittedly it is the very purpose of knowledge to know, since it cannot do this unless it knows immediately, and since what it knows, whether objects or 'ideas,' must be real in the sense of being actual, the only question possible is as to the *amount* and *kind* of reality which immediate consciousness discloses to our view.

My criticism, from this standpoint, is not single but twofold. As I have argued above, the subjectivists —Descartes is in this respect typical, as maintaining a thesis common to all subjectivists—while recognising that awareness must be immediate if it is to be possible at all, refuse to admit that in such awareness there is any genuine self-transcendence,[1] and therefore from the start they have committed themselves to the conclusion that the *sole* entities immediately apprehended are subjective in character. Though no attempt has been made to justify this assertion, it predetermines their conclusion. So much has, I trust, already been made clear. But I have also to pass a second criticism, namely, that Descartes and his successors—so far as they hold fast to his subjectivist thesis—have supposed that in accepting the occurrence of immediate knowledge they are likewise committed to the view that it is unanalysable. And

[1] This is, I think, no less true of Locke and Berkeley—their modes of speech notwithstanding—than of Descartes. Cf. above, p. 46 ff.

surely, it may be said, they are justified in this
belief! Can awareness be immediate, if it is not
also quite ultimate? And in its ultimateness, can
more be said about it than that it is what it is,
and does what it does, as vouched for by immediate
experience in ourselves and others? Is the asking
how awareness can be aware any better than the
inquiries how space is able to be extended, redness
red, or water wet?

Only a few words should be required to meet this
objection; it will be considered later in more detail.
I do not mean to criticise the subjectivists for regarding
awareness as an ultimate type of process. It is,
indeed, ultimate; [1] at least we must so regard it. Mr.
Dawes Hicks, in dwelling upon the fundamental
distinction between the two types of relation which
can hold between a physical thing and an act of
cognition, viz. as determining the act to occur and
as being itself cognised by it, adds the following
comment:

" The distinction coincides very largely with that which
Shadworth Hodgson was accustomed to draw between ' consciousness as an existent ' and ' consciousness as a knowing.'
Consciousness taken in the former sense, he used to argue, is
dependent upon neuro-cerebral processes which go on con-
comitantly with it, and to the question why it is that such
and such an act of perception occurs at such a time it is
legitimate to answer because such and such a neuro-cerebral
process has just taken place, or is taking place, at that time.
But, on the other hand, consciousness taken as a knowing—
the nature of consciousness, that is to say, which, however, he
regarded as made up of qualities that, for the most part, do not

---

[1] In describing it as ultimate, I do not mean that it is either indefinable
or unconditioned, but only that it does not belong to a genus of which
there are other known species.

seem to me to belong to it—can in no wise be said to be dependent upon the processes mentioned; we are wholly incapable of conceiving the character of consciousness *qua* character as caused in any way whatsoever. When we attempt to do so, we are really conceiving not the cause of the conscious state being *what* it is, but the cause of its happening or existence." [1]

With these remarks I can more or less agree. The nature of awareness cannot be observed from the outside, and its nature can never therefore be learned from study of the bodily processes which condition its occurrence. These latter (as all but the most extreme subjectivists agree in admitting) supply the supporting environment in which alone it is ever found; but study of them cannot supply the knowledge as to what it is that we must mean by consciousness. Such knowledge can be obtained only by actual participation in conscious awareness.

Yet when all this has been granted, it still remains true that awareness, however ultimate in type, must itself have a complex constitution, and that no theory of knowledge is adequate which fails to discriminate the various factors which go to compose it. This, as it seems to me, can only be denied so long as we fail to observe that meaning as well as fact is apprehended in every apprehended fact. If the field known be always of this character, must not the process of awareness, in order to be competent to its apprehension, be itself articulated in some corresponding manner? The problem cannot, indeed, be solved by the method of direct introspection—though the data supplied by introspection have to be taken into account—but only through study of what it is that awareness achieves.

---

[1] *Proc. Arist. Soc.*, 1916–17, p. 321.

But while this greatly adds to the difficulties which have to be overcome, it does not render them insuperable, and affords no kind of excuse for shirking the task. Those who do so are allowing unexamined assumptions to determine their premises, and so to decide their conclusions. This, at least, is what would seem to have happened in the case of those who have adopted a subjectivist position in any of its older, traditional forms. Their theory of knowledge, in its answer to fundamental problems, is—to repeat my previous form of words—little else than a re-statement in *subjectivist* form of that fundamental fact of *self*-transcendence which, in its initial, actually experienced, *realist* form, they have treated as paradox and as such refused to recognise. In ignoring, in their analysis of experience, the element of meaning, they ignore that very element through which alone the fact of self-transcendence can be rendered intelligible. For has not Kant, whatever his failures may otherwise be, succeeded in showing—so, at least, I should be prepared to argue—that the immediate is not a separate type of knowledge, but a factor itself conditioned by the presence and co-operation of other factors not so describable? But this is to anticipate: let us return to the discussion of those simpler issues which the subjectivists have themselves more or less explicitly recognised.

(ix.) A Twofold Conclusion

If we set aside these last-mentioned considerations, and review the road which we have thus far been travelling, we appear to arrive at a twofold conclusion. Subjectivism, in its traditional forms, has certain

F

radical, and seemingly fatal, weaknesses; but none the less it offers one great counter-advantage. Its defects are one and all traceable to its method of interpreting the cognitive situation. It repeats the 'dualism' which sets the problem—bringing 'within the mind' the primary distinction between knowing self and things known—and yet even by such extreme measures it fails to advance in any genuine manner our understanding of the issues involved. With one exception, the original difficulties of the situation continue unabated, and with certain others of a much more serious character superadded. The one exception is the counter-advantage to which I have referred. As we have noted, subjectivism would seem to render comprehensible the disparity which science discloses between the world as sensuously apprehended in a unique personal perspective and the world as impersonally and more adequately viewed in the natural sciences. If the secondary qualities, and consequently things as immediately experienced, are subjective existences, this disparity, it can be maintained, is understandable; whereas it is seemingly by no means easy of explanation on any view which retains the realist attitude of ordinary consciousness. This one great advantage of the subjectivist position has so outweighed all the theoretical objections, however logically unanswerable, which have been brought against it, that, as I have emphasised, it is the only theory of knowledge which has hitherto gained acceptance among non-professional students of philosophy. No matter how successful Kant and Hegel may have been in their critical handling of subjectivist teaching, their success in this direction has been more than counterbalanced by their failure to

provide any alternative position which is really work-
able and which is also compatible with the detailed
results of the physical and physiological sciences.
How far this defect is remediable we may now
endeavour to determine by a more detailed examination of the conditions and mode of existence of the
sensa.   Are we committed to the view that they are
mental in character?

CHAPTER V

THE NATURE AND FUNCTIONS OF THE SENSA

HAVING defined what I understand to have been the historical situation out of which the various present-day theories of knowledge have emerged, I shall, in what follows, leave aside all views alternative to those which I am myself endeavouring to establish, save in so far as consideration of these other views can be of assistance in developing my own argument. In this way I shall hope to be able to indicate much more effectually than by direct criticism the many respects in which I have been aided by, and those other respects in which I should dissent from, this and that type of realism and of modified representationism advocated in the recent literature of the subject.[1]

(i.) THE ONTOLOGICAL STATUS OF THE SECONDARY QUALITIES

What is the status of what are usually called the secondary qualities—colour, sound, taste, and the like?

---

[1] The two main types of what I should call ' modified representationism ' are those of Mr. Broad and of the authors of *Essays in Critical Realism* (1920). The criticisms which I should myself have been inclined to pass upon the latter have been very forcibly stated by Mr. Loewenberg in his ' Metaphysics of Critical Realism' (*Issues and Tendencies in Contemporary Philosophy*, Berkeley, 1923). Mr. Stout, as I understand, has now broken with representationism much more completely than in any of his published writings.

Upon what conditions do they rest, and can they be definitely classed either as physical or as mental?

We have already noted the ambiguity of the term sensation. It may mean either the process of sensing, *e.g.* the apprehension of red, or that which is sensed, *e.g.* the red itself. The latter we may entitle a sensum. Obviously the ' secondary qualities ' are not processes of apprehension; they are sensa.

Further, though the secondary qualities may perhaps turn out to be mental in character, there is no procurable evidence that they are states of the self. If by the self we mean the subject knowing, the sensa are not states of the subject, but objects to the subject. They are apprehended, *i.e.* contemplated. Pleasure and pain may perhaps be classed as states of the self: in so far as they are feelings they would seem to belong with processes of apprehension. Considerable special argument would, however, be required to show that we can interpret a taste or a sound or a colour in that manner. We can speak of the self (or mind) as pleased or pained or angry, but not as sweet or loud or red.[1] These latter qualities are contemplated, and though in the process they may awaken a subjective reaction, and so be appreciated, they are in themselves genuinely ' objective ' existences. As objects, they terminate the processes which are directed to their apprehension.

We must agree with the supporters of the doctrine

---

[1] Cf. Stout, *Manual*, 3rd edition, pp. 9-10, 112-15: " This relativity of affective values to the complex totality of our psychical life at the moment supplies a characteristic distinction between affective states and sensations which recur with comparative uniformity whenever a sense organ is similarly excited. Another characteristic difference is that distinct affective states are not capable of existing together in a simultaneous plurality as sensations are."

of representative perception that the sensa, *so far as experienced*, are transitory. They are experienced for a time, and then cease to be experienced. Whether they are in themselves transitory, coming into existence when we experience them and passing out of existence when we cease to experience them, we have no direct means of deciding; and the resulting questions raise many of the most difficult problems in metaphysics. The view to which, on general grounds, I find myself committed, is that they are events, and therefore, as capable of happening only once, essentially transitory. But since, like all events, they are ' slabs of duration,' [1] their duration need not coincide with our experiencing of them. For all that we know to the contrary, they may precede and outlast it, or may cease to exist before we have ceased to contemplate them.

Are the sensa likewise private to each individual? When a bell is rung, does each percipient in its neighbourhood receive therefrom his own separate set of auditory sensa? Or can the *same* sensa be apprehended by different percipients—uniformly in proportion as the conditions of location and hearing are uniform, and varyingly when these conditions vary?

In answer to these questions, three main attitudes can be adopted. First, there is the view taken by those who advocate the doctrine of representative perception, that the sensa are in all cases both private and subjective, *i.e.* are in their existence mind-dependent. This view we have already considered.[2] Secondly, there is the view taken by what may be called naïve realism, that the sensa actually exist, in the form in which they appear to exist, as qualities

---

[1] Cf. Whitehead, *The Concept of Nature*, p. 53.   See also below, p. 144 *n*.
[2] Cf. above, p. 18 ff.

of independent objects. This theory requires that we account for such facts as that blood should be red to the naked eye and yellow with red spots when seen through a microscope, that by the red-blind a red object should be sensed in some other colour, and so forth. But since this is the view taken, not only by ordinary consciousness, but also by such philosophical thinkers as Mr. Alexander and Mr. Percy Nunn, Mr. Dawes Hicks and Mr. Laird,[1] it cannot be lightly waved aside. A thorough discussion of the methods by which it has been defended would, however, take us very far afield.[2] I prefer to proceed by stating and developing the third remaining view, that the sensa are events, conditioned by physical, physiological, and possibly also (for deciding this point we have no sufficient data) psychical factors.[3] For the naïve realists the sensa are *public* and objective, whereas, on the view which I shall advocate, though objective, *i.e.* non-subjective, they are, for very sufficient, assignable reasons, open to the observation of only one percipient, and to that extent are *private*.

We may at once consider the main difficulty which stands in the way of this last view. Colour is, it would appear, apprehensible only as spread out, and

---

[1] Cf. Alexander, *Space, Time and Deity,* vol. ii. pp. 138-40; Percy Nunn, *Proc. Arist. Soc.,* 1909-10, p. 191 ff., and 1915-16, p. 156 ff.; Dawes Hicks, *Proc. Arist. Soc.,* 1916-17, pp. 342-4; Laird, *A Study in Realism,* pp. 36-44.

[2] Cf. Appendix to this chapter, below, p. 89.

[3] In the case of Mr. Alexander, the doctrine that sensory qualities are independently real is not incompatible with their being regarded as events. Mr. Alexander maintains that a quality *is* an event occurring within a certain set of events which constitute the thing qualified. On the other hand, he would not agree that sensa are *conditioned* by the physical and physiological factors involved in the processes of perception.

therefore as involving space. Must it not, therefore, be where the space is? Can colour be an event separate from extended existences, or have a set of conditions, physical and physiological, distinct from the conditions determining the existence of that of which it is the colour? By general admission our *apprehension* of colour is thus indirectly and complexly conditioned. Can this conclusion be extended to the existence of the colour itself?

In meeting this difficulty, I shall argue that the sensa reduce without remainder to the ' secondary qualities '; and that though space is apprehended *in terms of* sensa, it can never be apprehended *through* sensa. At this stage in our argument only part of the evidence for this position can be stated; its other grounds will be discussed in the succeeding chapters.

Mr. Ward and Mr. William James have argued that extensity is a characteristic of *all* sensa. There is, for instance, they contend, in sounds and tastes a voluminousness or roominess. The data upon which this view is based may, however, be taken as pointing in the opposite direction, as indicating that *none* of the sensa are *in themselves* extended, that all of them tend to *acquire* a seemingly direct relation to extension, and that in the case of visual sensa this has gone so far that colour cannot be consciously apprehended save as spread out. For do not the sensa of the special senses shade more or less continuously into the organic sensa? The order of sequence is indeed doubtful, since some of the organic sensa seem to suggest extensity more definitely than, for instance, sounds usually do. Still there is a marked difference between colours and sounds or odours, and the latter are in this respect more akin to the organic sensa than to our visual experiences. Visual sensa are but one type, and a somewhat exceptional type of sensa; and we may endeavour to treat them on the analogy of the other types, leaving their differentiating features for special explanation. Certainly, at least on first consideration, it seems more natural to treat tastes, odours, thermal sensa, sounds, and organic sensa, as suggesting extensity only through acquired associations, and as being, not qualities of objects, but events, conditioned by, and subsequent to, processes partly outside the body and partly within the body. On this view, sensa occur as terminating members in certain lengthy series of events which begin by being physical and become physiological.

Further, if this view be taken, separate sets of sensa must exist for each observer, since the sets of conditions upon which they follow are as distinct from one another as are the bodies of the percipients. This does not, however, mean that the sensa must be subjective, but only that they must be private. They are private, not because they fall outside the system of nature, but because, though in themselves as integral to nature as any other events, they are yet, owing to the circumstances under which they arise, accessible only to some one observer. Just as no two individuals can touch one and the same spot at the same time, or taste the same morsel of food, so no two observers can apprehend at any one moment, or even at different moments, the same sensa. They are, so to speak, in and by themselves just as public as any other natural existences; but owing to accompanying circumstances they are open only to some one individual's view, and so may be described as private.

If it be asked whether the sensa are physical or psychical, the answer will largely be a matter of convention, depending upon our definition of these terms. The term ' psychical ' is wider than the term ' conscious,' just as the term ' physical,' which applies to ether and to electrons, is wider than the term 'material.' The sensa cannot be shown to be *conscious* states, for by that we could only mean that consciousness is inseparably bound up with them; and in support of such a contention we have no sufficient evidence. Certainly their existence has never hitherto been demonstrated save on the direct testimony of immediate experience. When they are known to exist, consciousness is there bearing witness to their existence. But this is no proof that consciousness is what makes them possible of existence, and that they are unable to exist when consciousness is absent.[1]

Nor are data available for proving that the sensa are *mental* or *psychical* in any precise meaning of these terms. If we care to define the physical in a manner which excludes the sensory, and if we allow of no possible type of existence intermediate between the physical and the psychical, the sensa will have to be assigned to the latter class. But when we ask what grounds there are for excluding sensa from the physical sphere, none appear to be forthcoming save such as are bound up with those types of philosophy which have their sources in Cartesian ways of thinking, and which are therefore committed in one or another form to the doctrine of representative perception. In their attempts to define the relation of mind and body they have given rise to the current theories of interaction,

[1] On this general question, cf. G. E. Moore, *Proc. Arist. Soc.*, 1913–14, pp. 366-70.

automatism, and parallelism. As we have already noted, this way of thinking is mainly determined by the supposedly ultimate character of the physical teaching of Galileo and Newton; and so long as that teaching retains an unqualified prestige, such a view must appear to be inevitable. When, however, these views are challenged, several alternative possibilities at once open to our view. Thus if, as Whitehead contends in his *Concept of Nature*, the fundamental bifurcation is not between the psychical, taken as including the sensa, and the physical, taken as excluding them, but between awareness and a physical system of which the sensa are integral factors, the natural world will have to be envisaged in a very different manner from any anticipated in the traditional philosophies. If, further, we can follow Whitehead in his view that the fundamental natural concept is not that of substances but of events, and that correlation, not discernible continuity, is the only absolutely indispensable requirement in physical explanation,[1] the sensa, regarded as events [2] standing in definitely ascertainable correlations with physical and physiological events, will be factors as truly integral in the System of Nature as are any that are found in the inorganic world. Nature, on this view, becomes much more mysterious in character; fewer generalisations, not merely quantitative, are applicable to it; there are more loose ends; and new problems, not yet capable even of conjectural solution, open out on every hand. In particular, qualitative change, with all the difficulties

---

[1] Cf. below, pp. 172-5.

[2] I do not mean to imply that this is Mr. Whitehead's own view of sensa. He regards sensa as recognisable, recurring *objects*, *i.e.* as universals. Events, in contrast, are unique, non-recurring particulars.

which it involves, has now to be faced as a physical, not as a purely psychical, occurrence.

My statement that there is no sufficient evidence as to whether sensa do or do not have psychical conditions may seem to conflict with the contention that in any division of reality into the physical and the psychical they can most fittingly be classed as falling within the former. In reply, it may be pointed out that when the term psychical is employed in its widest sense as covering not merely awareness but all those powers and dispositions which constitute the mental structures of which awareness is a function, we are on debatable ground. In the absence of a metaphysical insight into the nature of the ultimate relations holding between mind and matter we have, perforce, to proceed in a tentative manner, and, as a first approximation to truth—to use the phrase now so frequently in the mouth of the scientist—may reasonably class the sensa as belonging rather to the physical than to the psychical sphere. If reality can be believed to be a system, and all its factors to be more or less integrally connected, an entity can be physical, and yet may be conditioned by what is different in nature from itself.

Further, even if it be granted that sensa do not as a rule rest on psychical conditions, we are by no means excluded from recognising, should evidence be forthcoming, that the psychical does yet in some degree determine the specific character which certain of the sensa are immediately sensed as having. Discussion of this question involves recognition of a distinction which I regard as quite fundamental, but to which I have not yet referred, between sensing and intuiting. By sensing I mean the process through which we apprehend the sensa, strictly so called, and by intuition the process through which we apprehend them in a spatial and temporal setting.   If, as I shall argue, the two processes, though fundamentally different and quite definitely distinguishable, never occur apart, they are likely to exercise influence on one another; and of their so doing there is a considerable amount of empirical evidence.   My treatment of the matter must, at this stage, be very incomplete; and I shall meantime leave aside all questions as to the interplay of intuiting and sensing.   In preparation, however, for the discussion of these questions in subsequent chapters, we may here consider certain more occasional, and, so to speak, superficial, interventions of the psychical factors.

The sense-qualities have developed in the phylogenetic process—such, at least, is the assumption which I am making—*pari passu* with the development of the sense-organs and of the parts of the brain with which the sense-organs connect.   That is to say, the sensa are, we may hold, complexly conditioned by inherited modifications in the structure, and consequently in the functioning of the nervous system.   It is possible that bodily modifications brought about in the course of the individual's experience are similarly efficacious, though in lesser degree, in determining what is sensed.   We have, however, no evidence to support such a conclusion.   On the other hand, we do find that certain of the sensa are conditioned by individual experiences which involve the element of *meaning*; and since this is an element for which it is difficult—we may even, relying on our present modes of insight, say impossible—to conceive any physiological counterpart, we would seem to be justified in concluding that certain of the sensa are in some degree *psychically* conditioned.[1] Evidence to this effect has been cited by Mr. Broad. After pointing out that the chief reason for regarding visual sensa as dependent on our bodies is that their variations then become intelligible as conditioned by the positions of the body, whereas the assumption that they depend on our minds gives no explanation whatsoever of such facts, he proceeds as follows:

" It does seem to me undeniable that in certain cases, and to a certain extent, our past experiences and our present expectations affect the actual properties of the sensa that we sense, and do not merely affect the judgments about physical objects which we base upon sensa." [2]

Take, for instance, the ' staircase ' diagram, given in psychological text-books as an instance of ambiguous figures:

" Its sensible appearance changes ' with a click,' as I look at it, from that of a staircase to that of an overhanging cornice. This change tends to take place as I concentrate my mind on the idea of the one or on that of the other. Now, on the present analysis of sensible appearance, such a change as this involves an actual qualitative change in the sensum. So far is it from being a mere change in the judgments which I happen to base on one and the same sensum, that the direction of my thoughts changes first and is the condition of the change in the sensible appearance." " The whole psychology of vision is full of such cases, some of them of a highly complex kind."

---

[1] Cf. Broad, *Scientific Thought*, p. 516: ". . . there may well be *purely* psychic conditions, having no bodily correlates, which must also be fulfilled if sensations are to arise in the mind. I am going to assume, for the sake of simplicity, in this book that there is such a complete parallelism between mind and body that it is enough to mention bodily conditions, because every psychic condition has its bodily correlate. I am very far from believing that this is *true*, and am not even sure that it has any very definite *meaning* which would survive analysis."

[2] *Op. cit.* p. 260.

" And it cannot be said here, as in the previous examples, that reference to the mind gives no help in explaining the facts Here the boot is rather on the other foot. . . . Here a reference to *mental* conditions really does explain concrete fact, whilst a reference to *bodily* conditions does not." [1]

If this type of argument can be upheld, and if, therefore, we can succeed in determining the progressive appearance, *in terms of* sensa, of factors which involve the element of meaning, we shall also be in a position to suggest an explanation of the manner in which the now inseparable connection between colour and extension has, in the course of the phylogenetic development, been brought about.[2]

Before concluding this section there is one other important consideration to which I may, in passing, draw attention; I shall have occasion to dwell upon it at some length later. On the above view of the sensa, the traditional manner of regarding the relation of mind and body will have to be restated, as involving two quite distinct problems.[3] For we shall have to ascribe to the brain a twofold function, as conditioning

---

[1] *Scientific Thought*, pp. 260-61. I cannot follow Mr. Broad in his further contention (p. 263, cf. 266) that " it is, of course, perfectly true that images are to a much greater extent qualitatively mind-dependent than are sensa." If I have not misunderstood him, he would here seem to be failing to distinguish between what determines the possibility of having images, viz. past experience, and what determines the character of the images once recalled. Since their occurrence depends upon our previous experience, they are much more under our control; but I can find no ground for believing that, once selected, by the direction of attention or otherwise, their qualitative characteristics are any less independent of mind than are those of the original sensa. They do not, it would seem, in the interval since our first experience of them, undergo any essential change, save perhaps diminution of their vividness and constancy.

[2] Cf. below, p. 200 ff.

[3] Mr. Stout has been the first to draw attention to this important point. Cf. his forthcoming Gifford Lectures.

the sensa and as conditioning awareness. Since these two functions are fundamentally distinct, there must be two sets of brain-processes; and they will call for separate treatment.

(ii.) TIME, SPACE, AND THE SENSA

Let us now consider the thesis which I have propounded above, namely, that we apprehend time and space *in terms of* sensa, but not *through* them, *i.e.* that we gain an articulated view of time and space by means of sensa, but that time and space are not themselves sensory in character. This can most easily be shown in the case of time. The passage of time is not, it would seem, absent from the field of consciousness for a single moment. It may not be specially attended to; it is at least ' enjoyed ' or ' endured.' Further, the time of which we are always thus conscious is, to use William James's phrase, a saddleback of time. What we are conscious of in being aware of succession is a duration within which we discriminate a past that has just passed, the now present, and a future into which it is leading. The present always defines itself in consciousness through this twofold contrast to the no longer and the not yet. Consciousness, that is to say, is never limited to the instantaneously present. In order that there may be consciousness of the present, there must be consciousness of more than the present. This, then, being the form in which consciousness of time alone occurs, I shall endeavour to show that it can never be acquired simply through contemplation of this or that sensum, as it comes about, as it endures for a time, or as it ceases to be, or even through contemplation of an overlapping series of such sensa.

Clearly, contemplation of a sensum in and by itself cannot yield, or account for, consciousness of its coming about. Since the awareness must take cognisance of the time prior to the happening of the sensum, it cannot be yielded by the not then existent sensum. Similarly with awareness of cessation of a sensum. The awareness is of a field which outlasts the sensum, and it must therefore apprehend more than the sensum. Consciousness of a continuing sensum is equally complex. It presupposes awareness of a lapse of time; and since it is the same sensum that is at the earlier and at the later time, the awareness of the difference in time cannot be obtained from contemplation merely of the sensum. Thus in all cases consciousness has a field more comprehensive than any sensum, no matter in which of the three modes the sensum be taken.

Nor can consciousness of time originate in the contemplation of overlapping sensa. If in their beginning and ceasing to be they entirely coincide, they begin and cease to be at the same moment, and the presupposed consciousness of antecedent time is not any more explained by them all taken together than it is by any one of them. If, on the other hand, the times of their beginnings stand in temporal sequence, and we date the later by reference to the earlier, then while awareness of the coming to be of the first item in the series is left unconsidered, and will call for parallel treatment, that of the subsequent items would seem to be accounted for. But this is an incomplete explanation. In order to date the later by reference to the earlier we must have ground for judging it to be later, and such ground can only consist in the awareness that it has really begun at the moment specified, that is, that it has followed upon a time in which it has not itself existed. And though this antecedent time may be apprehended as the time in which another sensum occurs, what makes possible the consciousness of the later item as *making its entry into* the series is consciousness of the preceding time as a *time* otherwise specified, not merely consciousness of the nature of the preceding sensum which does thus specify it. That is to say, in all cases awareness of a temporal field supplementary to this or that sensum, and in which the sensa occur, preconditions the apprehension of beginning, enduring, and ceasing to be.

To state the same argument in another form: in apprehending temporal overlapping of sensa we must apprehend the point or edge at which a new sensum begins or a given sensum ceases. But the edge is not apprehended as a temporal edge save in so far as it is viewed as occurring within a time that leads into and later continues the moment of transition in which the edge itself consists. More is here experienced than what is sensuously experienced. The time-span of known durations is what makes possible apprehension of a time-limit, and this time-span has itself to be thought of as continuing, and as continuing into, a time wider than itself.

But, it will be objected, the temporal contexts thus required can be explained as due to the revival of past experiences,[1] and so may still be traceable

---

[1] Kant, under the influence of those very assumptions from which he was endeavouring to break away, inconsistently adopts this method of explanation in his exposition of the ‘ syntheses of apprehension.’

to the contemplation of sensa. Examination of our consciousness of time suffices, however, to disprove this view. The type of context to which all such temporal contexts have to conform is a type which must in its main features be present in every case, and which is therefore as little capable of being accounted for in terms of past as in terms of present sensa. As conditioning *all* awareness of sensa, it cannot be arrived at through any amount of such awareness, not even if such awareness be thrown back into a past about which so little is known that con- jecture is free to propound hypotheses, uncontrolled by any facts of present experience. If, as above maintained, consciousness of the now cannot be accounted for save by postulating a consciousness of the no longer and the not yet, there can be no way of explaining how we can win our way to it by the path of increasing experience; and consciousness of duration must therefore be accepted as having been present from the start.

This conclusion can only be challenged if we are prepared to deny that consciousness, in order to be consciousness, must in all cases have a temporal field. The problem of the origin of our apprehension of time is the problem of the origin of consciousness itself.

Such, then, as regards consciousness of time, is the thesis which I am endeavouring to maintain. In order that what is sensuously experienced may be, what it always is, a complex duration, each item within it, and it itself as a whole, must be apprehended in temporal perspective. Only if the wider, *implied*, temporal perspective, and the time-span *immediately experienced*, be thus apprehended as passing into one

another, so that the texture of each is uniform in all
its transitions, can the changes which manifest themselves through the abrupt qualitative discontinuities
of sense still be apprehended in the manner in which
they are actually apprehended, namely, as constituting
a continuous medium of constant character. Accordingly, to explain consciousness of duration and
change, we have to postulate that the percipient is
capable of apprehending a wider, and in certain
respects, such as in the type of its continuity, a different
field from any that the sensa themselves, by themselves
(if they ever so exist), can be regarded as yielding.
Consciousness, in so far as it is the apprehension of
time and the modes of time, transcends any and all
sensa, however extensive, and however, *once they are
apprehended*, they may be found to be interpretable
as a *continuous* series of overlapping durations.

The same argument applies to our apprehension
of space. For even assuming (what I shall have to
call in question) that certain sensa, or all sensa, are
extended, there is one unfailing feature of our space-
experience which cannot be accounted for as due
merely to the contemplation of them as thus existing.
The space which we sensuously apprehend, be it large
or small, is always apprehended as falling within a
space larger than itself, and as being conditioned in
its existence by this wider whole. Consciousness of
such a field cannot be conceived as first originating
through observation of overlappings and delimita-
tions. That is necessary for definitely specifying any
space whether large or small, but will not suffice to
account for its first apprehension. The sensa have
indeed size and outline only in so far as they delimit
or overlap *one another*; but what makes it possible

that any two of them should be apprehended as thus co-terminous or overlapping is the single wider field within which both are located, and which thereby imposes conditions to which both must conform. Spatial limits, and therefore specific shapes and sizes, can be known only through a consciousness which *from the start* apprehends each of them in a wider unitary setting. The primary task of sense-perception is always—in space as in time—rather to differentiate than to synthesise.

Here, too, the remark made above in regard to time is in order. Not merely is the spatial context an *implied* wider context. While being so, it likewise with perfect continuity passes into, and maintains itself throughout, and emerges again beyond, the perceived space-span, and so enters into the very texture of what is immediately experienced in sensuous form. The field apprehended is thereby apprehended as fundamentally uniform in character, and when in mature consciousness it comes definitely to be recognised as all-comprehensive in its kind, has to be viewed as single. How this should be possible, and how in particular the sensa, notwithstanding their manifold and qualitatively discontinuous character, far from obscuring these features, should facilitate their apprehension, and in certain cases should themselves take on the spread-out form, remains a matter for later discussion.

There is, however, an objection of a related character, which may be considered in preliminary fashion before we proceed. Why, it may be asked, should we assume that the sensa are separate and unconnected? Is not any cogency the above argument may have entirely due to this false assumption? Do not the alleged difficulties at once vanish when we recognise that what we contemplate is a continuous field in time and space? If the field is in itself thus doubly continuous, does not this sufficiently explain why through direct inspection it is apprehended as being so?

I must refer the reader to the chapters that follow, but may meantime guard against certain misunderstandings which the objection would seem to involve. So far from meaning to deny that the sensuous field is always apprehended as continuous in time and space, I have myself been insisting upon this very fact. Consciousness, owing to sleep and other causes, may itself lapse, but the fields which it discloses to us, however circumscribed, and however lacking in *observed* continuity, in order to be apprehended as temporal and spatial, have to be apprehended (implicitly, if not explicitly) as selections from a whole which, without break, is continued into and continues them. I do, indeed, assume that the sensa are *qualitatively* discontinuous. This, as it seems to me, is an empirical fact, and must be accepted as such. The abrupt character of the transitions *from quality to quality* is surely a no less marked feature of the experienced than is the unfailing maintenance of continuity *in time and space.*[1]

I am also assuming that while all the sensa have duration, and so far exhibit temporal continuity, none of them, in and by themselves, possess spatial extensity. Whether this latter assumption is or is not justified, and how, if justified, the difficulties to which it gives rise are to be met, will have to be discussed later. At

---

[1] Whereas the relation between two distinct spaces or times is the space or time between the two, the relation between two sensa is not a sensum; *e.g.* the relation between two colours is not a colour, nor is it a sound.

present I desire only to point out that my argument, in the manner in which it is stated above, does not require, for its cogency, that we should deny the persistence of sensa in time. All that is demanded is that we recognise as a fact quite fundamental that the continuing character of sensa does not, by itself, suffice to explain consciousness of their continuity, and that this consciousness cannot therefore be due simply to direct inspection. I have tried to show that persistence, no less than change, involves for its apprehension a wider field than any or all simultaneous sensa can supply, and that even when previously experienced sensa are taken into account the temporal perspective necessary for the apprehension of any temporal relation remains unaccounted for. Accordingly, even if I were not questioning that extensity is a property of sensa, I should still have to apply the above view in explanation of our apprehension of space. What is true on the larger scale as regards the apprehension of this or that spatial field—that it cannot be apprehended save as part of a field still larger—is likewise true of the apprehension of any of its sensuously experienced parts: these can be so experienced *in terms of* sensa, only because very much more is involved than the sensa therein apprehended themselves make possible. This reply is no more than a repetition of my previous points, but it may serve to set them in a clearer light.

Mr. Stout has maintained,[1] though with a somewhat different purpose in view, a similar thesis,

Cf. *Manual,* 3rd edition, p. 431 ff; *Proc. Arist. Soc.,* 1914-15, Note on 'Knowledge by acquaintance' and 'Knowledge about,' pp. 350-51; *Some Fundamental Points in the Theory of Knowledge* (St. Andrews University Quincentenary Publications, 1911), p. 17 ff.; and more especially his forthcoming Gifford Lectures.

namely, that in all experience there is involved a form of knowledge which does not reduce to acquaintance or to acquaintance plus inference. This type of apprehension is, he maintains, an ultimate type: it cannot be acquired, and must be present from the start. As an instance he cites the apprehension of the past as past, and of all spaces as being parts of a single space. This position I should carry further, contending that these and other similar apprehensions, required in the apprehension of time and of space, together constitute that highly complex process which we entitle awareness. Since, as would appear to be an empirical fact, the minimum field is always both temporal and spatial,[1] and therefore elaborately complex, the awareness thereof is likely to be no less so. Those who regard extensity as a property of all sensa evidently intend to maintain that it is an ultimate and invariable feature of the *sensed*. For reasons which I shall proceed to state, while agreeing that time and space are for us ultimate features of *the real*, I cannot see my way to regarding them as sensuous. Nor can I agree that awareness of extensity is on all-fours with awareness of a ' quality ' such as red or sweet. This latter awareness appears to be unanalysable, but the awareness of time and space must surely have a complexity in some degree corresponding to the complex characters which it reveals.

[1] This is so even when we are attending to mental processes, since we cannot attend to them without also being aware of that to which they are directed, namely, the spatio-temporal.

APPENDIX TO CHAPTER V

Mr. Broad's Discussion of the Alternative Theories regarding the Production of Sensa

WHILE completing the above chapter I have become acquainted with Mr. Broad's very illuminating discussion [1] of the relative merits of the two main alternative views regarding the 'production' of sensations; and for the reader's benefit I here insert a brief statement of his argument.

The production of sensations (a term which Mr. Broad uses as signifying the complex within which sensing and a sensum can be distinguished) must be either *selective* or *generative*. Mr. Alexander is the most thoroughgoing representative of the former view. He regards sensa as contained in physical objects, and the physiological processes in the nervous system and brain as having, in this connection, only one function, that of 'keeping up' the mental process (or 'enjoyment') which senses, *i.e.* contemplates them. Objects have temperature, colour, and all their other qualities quite independently of their relation to any animal body or to any mind. The intervening processes, physical and physiological, determine which of these qualities we sense at any moment, but have nothing to do with their existence. Bodies which are literally red emit a positive type of physical vibrations; and these latter are the means of stimulating us to sense the red colour.[2] The vibrations, so far from being among the causal conditions of the existence of the colours, are part of the effects subsequent thereupon.

---

[1] *Scientific Thought*, p. 523 ff.   [2] Cf. *op. cit.* p. 280.

The alternative view is that the physiological processes have a further function, that of conditioning the *existence* of the sensa as well as that of conditioning our *awareness* of them.   This is the generative view which I have been advocating.   Sensa are the joint-product of physical and physiological processes, and possibly also of psychical processes.   We are not required, on this theory, to hold that sensa exist only in and through the processes whereby they are apprehended, nor to assert that they are non-physical.   But the theory does break with the selective view so far as to maintain that the probabilities are against the existence of sensa on the simpler inorganic level, and point to their being conditioned by physiological happenings.

Since there does not seem to be any direct method of deciding between the two theories, we have to do so by consideration of their respective advantages and disadvantages.

" [The] chief merit [of theories of the selective type] is that they make the ontological status of sensa easier to understand than do generative theories.   With the latter there is a sharp distinction between scientific objects and events on the one hand, and the sensa, which, under certain peculiar circumstances, they generate on the other.   The very notion of generation is not easy to understand, whilst that of selection is fairly intelligible.   And the status of sensa, when generated, in a world which consists almost wholly of scientific events and objects, is certainly most peculiar. . . .   On the view of physical objects and events which corresponds to the selective theory of the production of sensa, all that we need to postulate is unsensed sensa and unsensed sense-objects.   That is, we only need to assume more entities of the same kind as we meet in our sense-histories.

" Thus . . . if a *purely selective theory* can be made to work, and if it can be accompanied by a satisfactory theory of physical objects as composed wholly of sensa, it *will have the double merit of avoiding the difficult notion of generation and of giving sensa a less ambiguous status in the universe than any generative theory is likely to do."* [1]

But the difficulties in the way of a purely selective theory are no less obvious. For it constrains us to postulate a very grotesque type of complexity in the empirical objects.

" If physiological processes be purely selective, we shall have to postulate as many different kinds of sensa coexisting at a given place and time as any observer, however abnormal his bodily condition, can sense if put there at that time." [2]

For instance, the pushing of the eyeball aside with the finger brings two sense-objects into view where previously there was only one. If bodily conditions be purely selective, never generative, the two separate and similar sense-objects must have been there all the time.

" I find this very difficult to swallow; and a supporter of a purely selective theory will have to swallow a large number of equally unpalatable doses. If the sensa which an abnormal observer, or a normal observer in a temporarily abnormal state, senses from a certain place were *absolutely unlike* those which normal observers sense from that place, a purely selective theory would be more plausible. The difficulty is that the abnormal sensa are a great deal like the normal ones, and yet distinctly different. It is very difficult, under these conditions, to resist the conviction that both the abnormal and the normal sensa are *generated* by two sets of conditions, one common to both, and one varying from observer to observer." [3]

The range of this objection can be fully appreciated only when we bear in mind all the varied, relevant phenomena—negative after-images, dream-images, the

---

[1] *Scientific Thought*, pp. 526-7. Italics not in text.
[2] *Op. cit.* p. 528.   [3] *Op. cit.* p. 529.

varying shapes and sizes and colours of objects, the doubleness of all objects not on the horopter of vision, etc.

In view of the above considerations may not the most satisfactory solution be found in a combination of the two views?   Perhaps so; but in that case, as Mr. Broad points out, the selective theory loses many of its advantages.   If the internal bodily processes are allowed to be in any degree generative, even if only by acting in a manner analogous to distorting media, like coloured glasses, the limits within which this can occur will not be determinable.

" We therefore [should] not really know that sensa can exist at all apart from brains and nervous systems.   And, even if we decide to postulate sensa of *some* kind in places and times where there are no brains and nervous systems, we cannot have the slightest idea what intrinsic sensible qualities such sensa will have. . . . To call them *sensa*, under these circumstances, seems rather misleading; for it is liable to disguise the purely hypothetical character of these events and to suggest that we know a good deal about their intrinsic qualities.   Really we know nothing about the events which happen at intermediate times and places between the opening of a shutter and our sensing of a flash, except that they obey Maxwell's Equations." [1]

In any case, the admission of a power to alter, distort, and duplicate *is* the introduction of the concept of generation ; and, as Mr. Broad proceeds to show, the distinction between creative and causal processes is not an absolute one.   There are creative features in a so-called purely causal process, and there are causal features in the alleged generation of sensa.

" The difference may be stated shortly, in terms of occurrent and continuant conditions.   Both causation and creation involve

[1] *Scientific Thought,* pp. 532-3.

these two kinds of condition. In ordinary causation the event which is determined by them *joins up with* one or other of the continuant conditions, and becomes a part of *its* history. In creation, the event which is determined does not join up with any of its continuant conditions to form a further stage in their history; it either remains isolated or is the beginning of an altogether new strand of history." [1]

On the view that sensa are *generated*, they do not wholly fail to join up with pre-existing continuants.

"What we must say is that *sometimes* they seem to be extremely isolated; that *often* their connexion with pre-existing continuants is rather remote and indirect; and that apparently they *never* join up with the history of that particular continuant (viz. the brain) which is the seat of the most immediate special occurrent conditions. These facts show that the generation of sensa by physical and physiological processes must be considerably different from the causation of a change in one physical object by a change in another. But they do not suggest that the generation of sensa, if it take place at all, is a perfectly unintelligible process of creation." [2]

Similarly, the discontinuous, creative character is never wholly absent from strictly physical causation, though in the positive sciences it is more or less completely left out of account.

"We have no right then to feel surprised if the structure and laws of the existent world as a whole fail to show that sweet simplicity which distinguishes the particular part of it to which natural scientists have confined themselves. Science has been able to make the great strides which it has made by deliberately ignoring one side of reality. . . . In philosophy, as in economics, facts do not cease to be real by being ignored; and the philosopher becomes the residuary legatee of all those aspects of reality which the physicist (quite rightly, for his own purpose) has decided to leave out of account." [3]

---

[1] *Scientific Thought*, pp. 535-6.   [2] *Op. cit.* p. 539.
[3] *Op. cit.* p. 542. Cf. below, pp. 172-5.

Thus, though each of the two types of theory, the selective and the generative, has very serious difficulties to meet, both are open possibilities.   Our choice must depend partly upon our estimate of their respective successes in accounting for the main outstanding phenomena, and partly by the general views to which we find ourselves committed in treating of other problems in kindred fields.

CHAPTER VI

THE PRESENTATIONAL CONTINUUM [1]

I MAY render the above positions somewhat more definite by contrasting them with those of Mr. Ward and Mr. Stout. Though the views which I am advocating lead to conclusions very different from those of Mr. Ward, they are in some degree inspired by his teaching, and especially by his doctrine of a presentational continuum. A somewhat detailed statement and discussion of that doctrine would therefore seem to be called for.

(i.) A RESTATEMENT OF MR. WARD'S DOCTRINE OF A PRESENTATIONAL CONTINUUM

The doctrine had best be given in Mr. Ward's own words:

" Psychologists have usually represented mental advance as consisting fundamentally in the combination and recombination of various elementary units, the so-called sensations and primitive movements : in other words, as consisting in a species of ' mental chemistry.' If needful, we might find in biology far better analogies to the progressive differentiation of experience than in the physical upbuilding of molecules. The process seems much more a segmentation of what is originally continuous

---

[1] Should the reader prefer to keep to the main broader lines of the argument, he can omit this chapter and proceed at once to Chapter VII.

than an aggregation of elements at first independent and distinct. . . . In our search for a theory of presentations, then, it is from this 'continuity of consciousness' that we must take our start. Working backwards from this as we find it now, we are led alike by particular facts and general considerations to the conception of a *totum objectivum* or objective continuum which is gradually differentiated." [1]

" The notion—which Hume and Kant did so much to encourage—that psychical life begins with a confused manifold of sensations, devoid not only of logical but even of psychological unity, is one that becomes more inconceivable the more closely we consider it. An absolutely new presentation, having no sort of connexion with former presentations till the subject has synthesised it with them, is a concept for which it would be hard to find warrant either by direct observation, by inference from biology, or in considerations of a general kind." [2]

" The view here taken is (1) that at its first appearance in psychical life a new sensation or so-called elementary presentation is really a partial modification of some pre-existing and persisting presentational whole, which thereby becomes more complex than it was before; and (2) that this increasing complexity and differentiation never gives rise to a plurality of discontinuous presentations, having a distinctness and individuality such as the atoms or elementary particles of the physical world are supposed to have." [3]   " The pure sensation we may regard as a psychological myth." [4]

There appear to be two main reasons why this doctrine of a presentational continuum, though influential, has not been even more generally adopted. In the first place, Mr. Ward's professed intention is to describe the development of experience not only in the individual and in the race, but also in its evolution

[1] *Psychological Principles*, pp. 75-6. Cf. *Encyc. Brit.*, 9th edition, vol. xx. p. 45.
[2] *Op. cit.* p. 77. Cf. *Encyc. Brit., loc. cit.*, p. 45.
[3] *Op. cit.* p. 78. Cf. *Encyc. Brit., loc. cit.*, p. 46.
[4] *Op. cit.* p. 143. Cf. *Encyc. Brit., loc. cit.*, p. 53.

from the lowest forms of animal life. For this purpose Mr. Ward resorts to the assumption that we are dealing with one individual who is born as protoplasm and in the unbroken course of a single life develops into man.

"The life-history of such an imaginary individual, that is to say, would correspond with all that was new in the experience of a certain typical series of individuals each of whom advanced a certain stage in mental differentiation. On the other hand, from this history would be omitted that inherited reproduction of the net results of ancestral experience, that innate tradition, so to say, by which alone, under the actual conditions of existence, racial progress is possible." [1]

Now obviously a description which is thus to apply both to phylogenetic and to ontogenetic development must be very general; the phenomena covered are so multitudinous and diverse that only by departing from the above assumption, and by recognising the intervention of predispositions or powers, of which the psychologist is not yet able to give any specific evolutionary explanation, can any one stage, and especially the highly differentiated experience proper to man, receive adequate attention. And as a matter of fact, Mr. Ward frequently finds himself constrained to dwell upon this alternative type of problem. But even when he is doing so his fundamental assumption seems, at the really critical points, to exercise an unfortunate influence by diverting his inquiry from the specific phenomena under consideration to somewhat speculative conjectures as to the general mode in which they have been evolved from experiences simpler in type. In opposition to such a standpoint, we may welcome Mr. Stout's weighty pronouncement that in distinguishing between the

[1] *Psychological Principles,* p. 75. Cf. *Encyc. Brit., loc. cit.,* p. 45.

original and the acquired the psychologist should
mainly be concerned

" to guard himself against the danger of explaining in a circle
by unconsciously introducing among the essential conditions of
mental development what he pretends to account for as its
result. *To avoid fallacies of this sort it is best to err on the safe
side, if at all, and to rank as original whatever he cannot clearly
account for as derivative.*" [1]

There is little to challenge in the passages above
quoted from Mr. Ward, so long as they are taken as
applying to the broader features in the natural history
of the mind. The general point of view, as Mr. Ward
very justly claims, " has become the common property
of students to whom the original is unknown." [2]
When, however, we inquire in what precise respects
his description of the field of consciousness, the *totum
objectivum*, as being a continuum, can be accepted as
true of the field disclosed in our present human experience, objections multiply; and it is by no means
easy to discover what precisely Mr. Ward intends in
this connection. He does not mean that there are no
abrupt qualitative changes. A clap of thunder [3] can
break in upon silence; and lights can flash out against a
dark background. Neither the thunder nor the lights
are quite novel experiences, and all of them therefore
can be recognised; but there need be nothing like
them in the immediately preceding experiences. The
new presentations are indeed mediated by awareness of the transition-stages, thunder-*breaking*-in-upon-
silence, lights-*flashing*-out-against-darkness; but these
are only the processes whereby the abruptness of the

---

[1] *Manual of Psychology*, 3rd edition, p. 431.   Italics not in text.
[2] *Psychological Principles*, p. vii.
[3] *Psychological Principles*, pp. 77-8.   Cf. *Encyc. Brit.*, *loc. cit.*, pp. 45-6.

changes are apprehended, and whereby the changes,
once they occur, are experienced as progressively modifying the field into which they have unexpectedly
forced themselves.   There is always continuity in our
processes of awareness, even in the experiences of sur-
prise and disappointment; and had these processes a
wider presentational field, the thunder and the lights
would doubtless be anticipated before they occur, and
when occurring would be apprehended in the nexus of
the continuously changing physical occurrences with
which they are bound up.   The situation, however,
being what it is, the actual field is circumscribed, and
the sensations present themselves unintroduced, breaking the continuity of the experienced objective happenings, and substituting for qualities in the existing field
qualities of a quite opposite character.   It is not that
the previous processes are experienced as continuously
changing into something different: the changes are
experienced as in *contrast* to the immediately preceding.
The thunder does not, so to speak, begin as something
akin to silence and yet a little different from it, and
become its own self by continuous intermediate stages.

But if this be granted, what justifies Mr. Ward in
describing the presentational field as a continuum?
Seemingly only this, that the time and the space in
which its states and processes are apprehended are in
each case single and continuous.   There may also, as
Ward argues, have been continuity in the stages
whereby our qualitatively contrasted sense-experiences
have been differentiated out of the primitive presentational continuum of the protoplasm.   But this has
nothing at all to do with the question whether or not
in the complex field of any actual consciousness the
different factors are qualitatively continuous one with

another or with their immediate antecedents. The
continuity of the continuum, if we may trust introspection, lies exclusively in its temporal and spatial
aspects.

(ii.) An Examination of Mr. Ward's and Mr. Stout's Doctrine of Sensory Extensity

This, however, only brings us to a further, and
much more serious, difficulty. Mr. Ward has also
adopted the view, first propounded by Stumpf, that
extensity is apprehended in the same manner as
quality.

" In [our] sensations we can distinguish three variations,
viz., variations of quality, of intensity, and of what Dr. Bain
has called massiveness, or as we shall say, extensity." [1]

If this meant that each sensation has a space of
its own, it might be asked what in that case renders
the *totum objectivum* a *continuous* field? This, however,
is not what Mr. Ward intends to maintain. Notwithstanding his treatment of extensity as being on
a level with quality, he ascribes extensity to the field
as a whole, and *discriminates* the extensity of this or
that sensation within the single whole.[2] The extensities
of simultaneous sensations are, he virtually asserts,
partial extensities within the single extensity of the
presentational continuum. The chief relevant passages
run as follows:

" Intensity belongs to what may be called graded quantity:
admits of increment or decrement, but is not a sum of parts.
Nor is extensity, *as such*, a sum of parts; though it turns out

---

[1] *Psychological Principles*, p. 78.   Cf. *Encyc. Brit., loc. cit.*, p. 46.
[2] How large a spread-out extensity, uniform in quality, can be apprehended through a single sensation, is not discussed.

to imply plurality, since it can be differentiated. We might describe it as latent or merged plurality, or better still as a 'ground' of plurality.   In other words, to say that a single presentation has massiveness is the same as saying that a portion of the presentation-continuum, at the moment undifferentiated, is capable of differentiation—as happens, if for one of the two stamps the wet cloth is substituted." [1]

Without stopping to consider how far it is legitimate to ascribe to a single sensation [2] the extensity yielded by two stamps pasted side by side on the back of the hand, we may note that in the opening of the immediately following paragraph Mr. Ward, without any further attempt at argument, quite unambiguously assigns extensity to the field as a whole.

" Attributing this property of extensity to the presentation-continuum as a whole,[3] we have now to consider the relation of any particular sensation to this larger whole.   So long as the extensity of such sensation admits of diminution without the sensation becoming *nil*, so long the sensation either has or may have two or more so-called ' local signs.'   For what is gone—one of the stamps, *e.g.*, being removed—though identical in quality and intensity with what remains, will obviously *be* a different part of the whole.   But such difference of relations to the whole can only be regarded as affording a ground or possibility of local distinction, not as being from the beginning such an overt difference as the term ' local sign,' when used by Lotze, is meant to imply.   But we can say that more partial presentations are concerned in the sensation where there are two stamps than where there is only one.   The local differentia-

---

[1] *Psychological Principles*, p. 147.   Cf. *Encyc. Brit.*, *loc. cit.*, p. 54.

[2] By ' single presentation ' may be meant ' single presented field.'   If so, the difficulty is merely evaded.

[3] The sentence in its original more explicit form (*Encyc. Brit.*, *loc. cit.*, p. 54) is worth noting.   " Attributing this property of extensity to the presentation-continuum as a whole, we may call the relation of any particular sensation to this larger whole its *local sign*, and can see that, so long as the extensity of a presentation admits," etc.

tion of such compound sensation is what we have next to
consider or, in other words, the development of what Weber
called *Ortsinn*, local or topical sense." [1]

This last problem Ward proceeds to solve by the
aid of motor experience. But, as he is careful to
emphasise, all apprehension of space is bound up with,
and is only possible in terms of, the ' extensity of
sensation.'

"This much we may allow is original; for the longer we
reflect the more clearly we see that no combination or association of sensations varying only in intensity and quality, not even
if motor sensations were among them, will account for this
element in our spatial perception. . . . The most elaborate
attempt to get extensity out of succession and co-existence in
this way is that of Herbert Spencer. He has done, perhaps, all
that can be done, and only to make it the more plain that the
entire procedure is a ὕστερον πρότερον. . . . But, before and
apart from movement altogether, we experience that massiveness or extensity of impressions within which, *when it is
differentiated*, movements enable us to find positions, and to
determine distances." [2]

In the very beginning of experience, Mr. Ward
suggests,[3] every intense sensation would ' diffuse over '
the whole field apprehended, and only with increased
differentiation would restriction, and therefore the
apprehension of simultaneous differently located areas,
come about.

[1] *Psychological Principles*, p. 147. Cf. *Encyc. Brit., loc. cit.*, p. 54.
[2] *Op. cit.* pp. 145-6. Cf. *Encyc. Brit., loc. cit.*, p. 53.
[3] *Op. cit.* pp. 79-80. Cf. *Encyc. Brit., loc. cit.*, p. 46. Cf. the sentence added in *Psychological Principles*, p. 79 : "As already said, the very
beginning of experience is beyond us, though it is our business—
working from within—to push our analysis as far as we can." The
fundamental fact which Ward has here in mind, and which is vouched
for by *present* experience, is that, "even at our level of mental evolution,
an increase in the intensity of a sensation is apt to entail an increase in
its extensity too."

" These processes have now proceeded so far that at the level of human consciousness we find it hard to form any tolerably clear conception of a field of consciousness in which an intense sensation, no matter what, might—so to say—diffuse over the whole.   Colours, *e.g.*, are with us so distinct from sounds that—except as regards the excitement of attention or the drain upon it—there is nothing in the intensest colour to affect the simultaneous presentation of a sound.   But, at the beginning, whatever we regard as the earliest differentiation of sound might have been incopresentable with the earliest differentiation of colour, if sufficiently diffused; much as a field of sight all blue is now incopresentable with one all red. . . . Now, on the other hand, colours and sounds are so far localised that we may be directly aware that the eye is concerned with the one and the ear with the other."

Quite evidently this passage is inspired by the conviction that there is but one single field apprehended.   Otherwise it would be meaningless to speak of ' diffusion ' or ' radiation ' ' over the whole '; and there would be no ground for alleging that, since different sensations cannot, without blending, extend over the same whole, they must for this reason, until ' restriction ' comes about, be incopresentable. ' Diffusion ' is a metaphor [1] which is only applicable where there is an independently existing field throughout which, or over which, the diffusion can take place.   The term reappears in Mr. Stout's account of the manner in which, through local signs,[2] the extensities of our sensa are co-ordinated and internally developed. Mr. Stout is, however, so far justified in using this form of words, in that he does not regard the local sign sensations as possessing extensity but as fusing

---

[1] That Mr. Ward is not unaware of this, is shown by his having added to the original wording of the *Encyclopædia* article the phrase ' so to say.'

[2] Cf. *Manual*, p. 466: " Extensity is nothing but the continuous repetition or diffusion of local sign difference."

with the extensities of the fundamental sensations, tactual or visual, which they accompany.

Now how are we to combine the two contentions (1) that extensity is a property of the presentational continuum as a whole, and (2) that extensity is a property of sensation? Must not Mr. Ward either hold, with greater consistency, to his thesis that "pure sensation is a psychological myth" and therefore incapable, in and by itself, of constituting an extensive field, or else be prepared to sacrifice his doctrine of the presentational continuum? The general trend of his argument is overwhelmingly on the lines of the former alternative, whereas Mr. Stout seems quite definitely to have decided for separate and independent extensities peculiar to this or that sensum.

The issue is complicated by Mr. Ward's insistence upon a distinction between extensity and space—a distinction which Mr. Stout retains, and which figures prominently in his analysis of space-perception.[1] If Mr. Ward means only to distinguish between space as immediately apprehended and this same space as interpreted in conceptual terms, there can be no question. The former is concrete and personal; the latter, on the other hand, is at once abstract and ideal. Mr. Ward asks us [2] to consider the difference between the twelve-foot wide ditch for a traveller who can clear it by a jump and for the traveller who must halt on its brink. So, too, the concrete ' up ' is much more than a different direction from ' along.' Further, in the concrete, the body is the datum to which all positions are referred, and such positions differ not merely geometrically but qualitatively.

[1] Cf. above, p. 50.
[2] *Psychological Principles*, p. 144.   Cf. *Encyc. Brit., loc. cit.*, p. 53.

" It is a long way from these facts of perception, which
the brutes share with us, to that scientific concept of space, as
having three dimensions and no qualitative differences, which
we have elaborated by the aid of thought and language; and
which reason may see to be the logical presupposition of what
in the order of mental development has chronologically pre-
ceded it." [1]

But Mr. Ward offers yet another type of reason
which is hardly compatible with this method of distinguishing between extensity and space. Space, he
points out, is complex, involving a plurality in relations
of externality, juxtaposition, distance, etc., and, I may
add, forming in terms of these relations a continuum
of a highly specific type. This complexity alone
would, Mr. Ward says, suffice to show that space,
unlike extensity, is certainly not " psychologically *a
priori* or original in such sense that it has been either
actually or potentially an element in all presentation
from the very beginning." [2]   But is not this a doubtful
assertion? Does it not beg the question at issue? If
such complexity, even as 'implicit,' is inconsistent with
human experience, must not extensity be so likewise?
For does not extensity itself involve plurality and a quite
specific type of continuity? And has not Mr. Ward,
in his *Psychological Principles*,[3] himself come forward
as a defender of the *initial* complexity of the first
beginnings of human consciousness—the psychoplasm
in which the individual consciousness originates
having, he maintains, a complexity analogous to that
of its physical counterpart, the bioplasm?

[1] *Psychological Principles,* p. 145. Cf. *Encyc. Brit., loc. cit.,* p. 53.
[2] *Encyc. Brit., loc. cit.,* p. 53. In *Psychological Principles,* pp. 144-5, the
passage is altered in certain minor ways: *e.g.* ' implicitly or explicitly ' is
substituted for ' actually or potentially.'
[3] P. 412 ff. Cf. below, pp. 185-6.

The main, and ultimately, so far as I can see, the sole possible argument in support of a radical distinction between extensity and space is that which follows when extensity is taken, as by Mr. Ward and Mr. Stout, not as being a property of the real independent world but as belonging to a sensum or set of sensa, and the various extensities as therefore being originally independent and unconnected. Both Mr. Ward and Mr. Stout give, indeed, the further argument that extensity, as thus belonging to sensation, varies according to the standpoint, etc., of the percipient, whereas space is an attribute of bodies, and does not alter. Both this and the preceding argument are, however, bound up with the theories of perception which they respectively hold, and presuppose the truth of the controversial doctrines upon which these theories rest.[1] While no one can deny the quite obvious differences between our initial experiences of extensity and the mathematical conception of the nature and properties of space, the continuity of development upon which Mr. Ward is so insistent, and which leads him to rule out as incredible any primitive apprehension of space, can quite as easily lead—when we start not from conjectural views as to the beginnings of conscious experience but from present human experience—to the contrary conclusion. At least, since the principle of continuity can thus be worked from both ends, Mr. Ward's line of argument, when not otherwise reinforced, is decidedly precarious. And it is surely significant that Mr. Stout, who starts with a non-spatial extensity—if such a phrase be allowable—has, in order to make

---

[1] I have already commented upon Mr. Ward's distinction between sensory extensity and public space, above, p. 50.

possible the transition from earlier to later experience, to postulate *as present from the start*, a category
of spatial unity.[1]

Mr. Stout's own doctrine of extensity is as follows :
In the first place, he does not hold that *all* sensations
have extensity. Consequently he is able to adopt a
different view of ' local signs ' from that propounded
by Mr. Ward. The latter, as already stated,[2] in
accordance with his view that *all* sensations have
extensity and with his doctrine of a presentational
continuum, holds that the local sign of any particular
sensation is its relation to the continuum as a whole,
i.e. that there are not separate sets of sensations
which act as local signs. For Mr. Stout, on the
other hand, the local signs consist in " a certain
unique and ultimate diversity between simultaneous
sensations,"[3] apprehended in connection with *each*
experience of extensity. These local sign sensations
differ, apparently, from the sensations which have
extensity, not only in the absence of extensity, but in
not depending upon any assignable difference in
quality or intensity of stimulus. They depend on
differences in the manner in which locally distinct
parts of the sensitive surface of the body are connected
with the central nervous system.

There is demanded, however, a further condition;
and it is in the statement of this further condition
that the main characteristics of Mr. Stout's doctrine
come to view. Mr. Stout is proceeding to show how
by the aid of local sign presentations we locate
sensuously given extensities on this or that part of
the surface of the body, and also discriminate within
a given extensity the relative positions of its parts.

---

[1] Cf. below, p. 110.   [2] Cf. above, p. 100 ff.   [3] *Manual*, p. 216.

" Visual as well as tactual sensations have well-marked local signature. We can distinguish a patch of white on the left margin of the field of view from an otherwise similar patch of white on the right margin. The two light-stimuli affecting separate parts of the retina do not combine to produce a single sensation of greater intensity than either would occasion by itself, as would happen, for instance, in the case of two simultaneous sounds of the same quality. On the contrary, they produce two sensations distinguished by diversity of local sign." [1]

Now here, presumably, the two patches of white which we thus in experience distinguish from one another are, by differences in their local signs, prevented from combining to produce a single sensation. These differences, however, are not themselves spatial but only qualitative. On this view, therefore, all that we should experience are two extensities differentiated in a purely qualitative manner. No explanation has yet been given why they should be apprehended as spatially external to one another. Unfortunately, when Mr. Stout proceeds to deal with this all-important point he drops one of the two patches of white, and so simplifies his problem by the assumption that spatial relations are discriminated within the given extensity of a single sensation.[2]

" When I see a patch of white . . . I experience a complex of sensations differing in local sign. If, now, I attempt to analyse such a complex into its component parts, I find that each discernible part runs into and is continued into others; the ending of each is the beginning of another. In other words, the whole is sensibly continuous—an unbroken unity." [3]

---

[1] *Manual*, p. 216.

[2] Nor do I find the question answered in the later chapter devoted to the subject of visual perception.

[3] *Manual*, p. 216.

It is not entirely clear what is here being asserted. Is it simply the local signs that qualitatively shade continuously into one another? If so, the sensible continuity is only that of a qualitatively graduated series, and is not in any respect a spatial or extensive continuity. If, on the other hand, as the term ' discernible part ' would rather seem to imply, the continuity thus sensibly apprehended is extensive, how come the qualitative differences in the local sign sensations to signify *spatial* differences? Doubtless this is a difficulty which in one form or another arises on any theory as to how quality and extensity are interconnected; but as the local sign sensations [1] have been postulated for the very purpose of explaining the apprehension of spatial differences, the demand for a more definite answer than is here given is surely not unreasonable. But in any case, even granting the sufficiency of the above explanation, it is clear that the *continuity* of the diverse parts of space, and as involved therein awareness of its being a whole relatively to its parts, must be due to the initial, purely sensory experience of extensity. This is made even clearer by Mr. Stout's next sentences:

" Finally I reach a limit in the process of subdivision where I can no longer make explicit distinctions at all. *I am still aware of an extensive whole*; but I cannot pick out its parts severally for separate consideration. I am aware of the parts only implicitly in being aware of the whole containing them." [2]

That Mr. Stout, in defending his doctrine that extensity is a property of sensation, takes a very liberal view as to what may constitute a single sensa-

---

[1] Mr. Stout postulates these for sight though he admits that we have no introspective evidence of their existence.

[2] *Manual,* pp. 216-17. Italics not in text.

tion, appears from such a passage as the following. After referring to our experience of two contact sensations, and consequently of *apartness*, when the two points of a pair of compasses touch the skin at a sufficient interval, he proceeds:

" But when the points lie nearer to each other this is not so. We then fail to single out separate contact-sensations from the whole tactual presentation.   None the less, our sense-experience is not the same as it would be if only one compass-leg touched the skin.   *The sensation due to the double contact* is more extensive or diffused.   It is blurred, spread out, and referred to a wider area.   The local sign differences are therefore still present, though they are not separately singled out.   That they are really present is shown by the fact that it is frequently possible to discern the two touches separately when the compass-points are applied successively instead of simultaneously.   This is especially easy when the first point is removed before the application of the second." [1]

Apparently Mr. Stout is prepared to maintain that this sensuous experience of extensity is possible independently of the employment of any categories. In so far, however, as the mind also apprehends space (as distinguished from extensity), that is, an extended world, certain *a priori* categories are, he contends, quite indispensable; and among these he includes what he entitles the category of spatial unity.

" At our present level of mental development, spatial unity means that all extended bodies are extended in one and the same space, which is definitely contrasted as a whole with particular extensions as its parts.   When we perceive, imagine, or conceive any particular extension, we think of it as continued beyond itself, so as to be an inseparable portion of the one all-embracing space." [2]

---

[1] *Manual*, p. 217.   Italics not in text.
[2] *Op. cit.* p. 438.

Also the space thus apprehended is tri-dimensional:

" The apprehension of space as tri-dimensional is directly bound up with the category of spatial unity. . . . From the outset the apprehension of a third dimension is involved in the apprehension of surfaces. . . . Any given surface is thought as prolonged beyond itself ; and it is not only thought as prolonged into a further surface but also into extension which is not superficial." [1]

While thus maintaining that the category of spatial unity is involved in the apprehension of space, though not in the apprehension of extensity, Mr. Stout adds that he does not mean to imply that the sensuous level ever exists apart from the perceptual.

" If there is a stage in which the mind is aware only of its own sensations, it does not seem possible to point to any known psychological processes by which this stage could be transcended . . ." [2] " [Consequently] we must assume from the outset something answering, in however vague a form, to our developed consciousness of the world as a unity—a system within which all parts are in various ways connected with each other." [3] " Now we cannot, of course, attribute to the undeveloped consciousness the full and articulate consciousness of the unity of space which we possess ourselves.   None the less if we are to advance securely in our psychological explanation, it would

---

[1] *Manual*, pp. 439-40. Mr. Stout similarly postulates a category of temporal unity (p. 440) *but without distinguishing between ' protensity ' or duration and real time.* " What we assume under this head is that any particular duration or change is, from the outset, apprehended, however vaguely, as having a ' before ' and ' after.' In early stages of mental development, owing to the dominance of direct practical interest, the mind is preoccupied with continuation into the future rather than the past. Such reference to the future seems involved even in the most rudimentary forms of the attention process as indicated by the behaviour of animals and children. Even the most primitive attention is essentially prospective; it is a waiting or watching, a being on the alert for what is to come. . . . In other words, the reference to the future must be as primitive as conative consciousness."

[2] *Op. cit.* pp. 431-2.   [3] *Op. cit.* p. 438.

seem that an embryo form of it must be present from the outset
as the condition of further growth." [1]

If Mr. Stout be prepared to go as far as this, is he
not in consistency bound to go yet further, and to
recognise that the category of spatial unity is involved
in the apprehension of extensity, and that his distinction between extensity and space, when taken as
a radical one, is therefore untenable?   For must not
the category, if it is to achieve the purpose for which
it is postulated, do more than merely lead us to *think*
each given extensity as being a portion of a single
and all-embracing space?   What has to be accounted
for is our *perception* that the various discriminable
extensities do actually form parts of the total field of
the moment.   We do not merely *think* each of these
partial extents as belonging to a single space; we
sensuously *perceive* them as a continuous whole.
This whole we have indeed likewise to conceive as
forming part of a still larger whole.   But the spatial
unity must be intuitively apprehended if it is to be
conceived as being thus continued beyond itself; and
this surely is already done in the apprehension of
extensity.   In virtue of its continuity—intuition of
which, as I shall try to show in the next chapter, presupposes the employment of the categories—it is
only apprehensible as continued into, and therefore
as forming part of, space as a unity.[2]   The conceptual
elaboration of space in abstract thought can do no
more than body forth the actual nature of that very
extensity which we intuite in our sense-experience.

[1] *Manual,* p. 439.
[2] *Op. cit.* pp. 216-17.   Cf. p. 466 : " Extensity is nothing but the
continuous repetition or diffusion of local sign difference."

(iii.) Mr. Alexander's Distinction between Sensing and Intuiting

Though Mr. Alexander does not hold that the intuitive apprehension of space presupposes the categories, he insists upon the fundamental importance of the distinction between sensing and intuiting, and defines that distinction in the following terms:

" The primary qualities which are empirical differentiations of Space and Time never reach our minds, as Berkeley saw, except along with secondary ones. . . . But though our experience of Space and Time is thus provoked in us through sensation it does not follow and it is not the case that they are apprehended by the senses." [1]   " Every sensory act contains in itself, and consequently conceals or masks, a simpler act of intuition." [2] " It follows that when I see a blue patch I see its blue quality, but I have an intuition of its extent.   I do not see a blue which possesses an extent but I intuite an extent of space which I see blue.   I do not apprehend an extended colour but a coloured extent." [3]

As Mr. Alexander proceeds to show, this point of view has in especial, in its bearing on the theory of knowledge, one great advantage.

" If we suppose that our colours are extended and our touches also, we are faced with the problem of correlating the spaces of vision and of touch.   They are, in that case, as Berkeley rightly held, distinct spaces, and they do but get connected by custom, though it is difficult to understand how. Now if extent does not belong to colour as such, but colours are seen in their places within an extent, and the like is true of touch, it follows that when we apprehend the same object by sight and touch we are apprehending the same extent, and in the one case seeing its colours and in the other feeling its press-

---

[1] *Space, Time and Deity*, vol. ii. p. 143.
[2] *Op. cit.* ii. p. 148.   [3] *Op. cit.* ii. p. 164.

ures. . . . There are not two distinct spaces which have to be connected by custom or otherwise, but one space which is the scene of different qualities. . . . Instead of having a variety of different spaces which we never can make one, except by assuming some space not given in experience which is the condition of all these various spaces, our intuitive apprehension of things supplies us with the identical framework of a piece of space, within which the sensible qualities of the things are found." [1]

This position likewise possesses the supreme advantage, that it does not introduce between the mind and real space any intermediary, sensuous or otherwise. It is not argued that intuition is a more direct form of apprehension than the act of sensing,[2] but only that its objects, space and time, possess a constitution different in character from any sensuous quality, and such as allows of their being the fundamental features of a public world that is independently real.

(iv.) MR. RANDLE'S ANALYSIS OF SIZE-DISTANCE PERCEPTION

While engaged in writing the above I had the good fortune to come upon Mr. H. N. Randle's very interesting article, recently published in *Mind*,[3] on " Sense-Data and Sensible Appearances in Size-Distance Perception." Mr. Randle's main thesis is identical with Mr. Ward's contention that " pure sensation is a psychological myth," and is likewise inspired by Mr. Ward's own fundamental conviction

---

[1] *Space, Time and Deity*, vol. ii. pp. 164-5.   Cf. Mr. Alexander's valuable discussion of counter-views and of Dr. Head's more recent investigations, ii. pp. 165-74, 178-82.

[2] Cf. *op. cit.* ii. p. 147 *n.* " Intuition is no more direct than sensation and thought. All our apprehensions bring us face to face with their objects."

[3] Vol. xxxi. No. 123, July 1922, p. 284 ff.

that the presentational field is at every moment a single whole. But Mr. Randle has developed the thesis with such thoroughness and consistency that the terms in which it is formulated can be taken in a more literal and precise sense than Mr. Ward himself ever ventures to assign to them. Is sensation, Mr. Randle asks, the doorway of knowledge? And if it be so, can the world be kept at its proper distance from us, as a real and genuinely independent world? Is there indeed any such entity as sensation? These are questions directly relevant to our inquiry, and Mr. Randle, as it fortunately happens, has chosen to discuss them with special reference to the perception of magnitude, that is, of extensity. Those points in his argument which bear on the problems before us I shall briefly summarise.[1]

Sensation, or sense-datum, is usually taken as being a psychical entity corresponding to an elementary physiological process; and while it is generally granted that it cannot be experienced in purity, it is supposed to be discernible as an element within the field perceived. Now if extensive magnitude be a property of sensation, and be revealed in and through sensation, it ought to be thus detectable, as a something fixed and given.[2] But, as we find, it varies freely, independently of what is happening in the retina.

" Produce an after-image of the sun and look at your fingertip; it will be smaller than your nail. Project it on the table, and it will be as big as a strawberry; on the wall, as large as

---

[1] I shall have to omit his argument in favour of the non-subjectivity of ' perspective appearances.'

[2] Mr. Randle's argument proceeds, it may be observed, on the assumption that Mr. Ward's distinction between extensity and space is untenable. I have already commented on that distinction, above, pp. 50-52, 104 ff.

a plate; on yonder mountain, bigger than a house. And yet it is an unchanged retinal impression." [1]

And what here occurs is not the exception, but the rule. When, as ordinarily happens, the entire retina is affected, we see now one size of field and now another—an open book on the table before us, or miles of country, as the case may be—and everything in each field varies with the field as a whole. We shall therefore seek vainly for any size as ' given,' prior to the interpretation whereby the field seen is determined to be of this or that kind. When we look at the moon through a telescope, the moon stimulates an extent of retina many times larger than when we look at it with the naked eye, and yet it is a smaller, not a larger, moon that is then apprehended.

How have psychologists interpreted this last instance so as to harmonise it with their assumption of given sensuous extensities? By means of two sub-conscious inferences, sequent to one another,[2] and such that the second denies the premiss upon which the first is based.

" The case is analysed thus: (1) the actual retinal image is, and is seen as, larger; (2) as an effect of this, we judge that the moon is near; (3) this judgment of nearness makes us see the thing smaller—because if the moon is so near as it seems it must really be quite small, or its retinal image would be enormously bigger. It is supposed, in fact, that the ' sensation' corresponding to the magnified retinal image gives rise to a

[1] W. James, *Principles of Psychology*, vol. ii. p. 231. Quoted by Randle, p. 285. On this general question, cf. also Broad, *Scientific Thought*, p. 291 ff:, especially p. 297.

[2] Mr. Stout, I understand, would not agree to this statement; he would hold that apparent size and distance are determined together, in correlation with each other, as the resultant effect of all relevant factors (including extensity) in co-operation.

judgment of nearness; and that this judgment of nearness then destroys its own cause, the sensation of largeness, and generates in place of it a perception of smallness." [1]

A similar explanation is given of the varying sizes of the moon seen at the horizon and at the zenith. At the horizon, owing to the intervention of numerous objects in the intermediate field, to dimness of colouring, etc., we infer that it is distant; in consequence of this inference we see it as large; and seeing it as large, we infer that it must be near.

" This amounts to a chain of percepts each determining the next in the series, with an absurd result. Now there is no introspective evidence that we see the moon distant; and if we did, it would be psychologically impossible at the same time to see it near. The only possible result of such a rivalry of perceptions would be an alternation of the competing percepts, with a moon dancing a very disconcerting to-and-from *coranto* on the horizon." [2]

As Mr. Randle justly remarks, " such epicycles of explanation," " this amazing tissue of lies in the soul," are required only if we insist upon buttressing up the fundamental assumption that we immediately (though it may be subconsciously) apprehend each item in the visual field as having a *given* magnitude, and that we then proceed, by subconscious processes, in the light of previous experience, to alter and transform these magnitudes. There is, it would seem, but one explanation which will fit all the facts; and it is an explanation which, so far as regards extensive magnitude, allows of no fixity that is purely sensuous. Magnitude, though, of course, in part determined by retinal processes, is also, and mainly, determined by those factors which prescribe this or that meaning to

[1] Randle, *loc. cit.* pp. 293-4.   [2] Randle, *loc. cit.* p. 297.

the field as a whole.   Singleness or unity is an unfailing characteristic of the field apprehended, and
according as it is of this or that kind it constrains its
constituents to conform to its demands.[1]   The psychologist must break with merely physical metaphors, and
on the analogy of present-day physiological theory
conceive the mind as functioning in an integrative
manner.   We must postulate 'a schema or unconscious disposition'[2] which, in conditioning our conscious processes, determines them to the apprehension
of a complex and relatively definite field, characterised
throughout, in its wholeness and in its parts, by
sensuous magnitudes appropriate to its type.

What other explanation will fit the facts?   The
moon as seen through a telescope is small because the
telescope causes a collapse of planes.   The moon then
reduces automatically to the scale of the new perceptual schema.   "The moon projected on a nearer
plane is the moon of a smaller world, and so suffers
shrinkage to match the world, of which it is a function."[3]   Similarly the moon looks bigger on the
horizon because the over-arching heaven, being a much
flattened dome, demands as its correlate a smaller moon.
"The changes in the perceived size of sun and moon,

[1] Instances of this are cited by Stout in another connection.   Cf. *Manual,*
pp. 469-70.
[2] Cf. Myers, *Text-Book of Experimental Psychology,* 1911, pt. i. pp. 282,
293-4, quoted by Randle (p. 296): "Possibly we have here a schema or
unconscious disposition in regard to the distance of objects.   And when
this schema undergoes change, it manifests itself in consciousness by effecting
a change in apparent size, whereupon the apparent size determines our
awareness of the distance of the object."   Dr. Head has drawn attention to
the part played by 'schemata' in the recognition of posture and of the
locality of affected parts of the body: cf. *Brain,* vol. xxxiv. (1911–12),
pp. 185-9, reprinted in *Studies in Neurology* (1920), pp. 604-8.
[3] Randle, *loc. cit.* p. 294.

as they climb the zenith and descend again, are pro-
portional to the flattening of the arch."[1]   Signs of
distance, no less than extent of actual retinal impression,
here play their part, but in subordination to the all-
controlling influence of the wider schema within which
they function.   This explanation finds striking con-
firmation in the behaviour, as above noted, of after-
sensations.   Their size, *as initially and immediately
experienced*, is a function of the background against
which they are apprehended.[2]

There is, it may be noted, one fundamental respect
in which the traditional theory agrees with Mr.
Randle's.   What is undeniable—whatever our other
views may be—is the extraordinarily variable character
of extensive magnitudes, according as this or that
' interpretation ' is given to them.   They may, once
they are consciously apprehended, resist further
modification.   Though we may know that the moon
is no larger at the horizon, we continue to see it so.
None the less we cannot dispute that interpretation
counts among the conditions of sensible magnitude.
The two theories are at variance only in regard to the
pre-conscious agencies to which the variations are
due.[3]   *Qualitative* differences, *e.g.* between colours or

---

[1] Randle, *loc. cit.* p. 295.

[2] Stout's comment on the behaviour of the after-sensations is as follows:
" Where the varying distance of an object is fixed by other means, the extent
of the retinal impression mainly determines perception of magnitude.   This
is well seen in the case of after-images."   And, after quoting the above
passage from James, he proceeds :   " An actual thing producing a retinal
excitation of the same extent would vary in size according to distance.
Hence the *imaginary* thing *suggested* by the after-image *appears* of different
sizes, when it is perceived at different distances.   But the actual retinal
sensation is in all cases the same " (*Manual*, pp. 502-3).   Italics not in text.

[3] This last statement is, of course, valid only in so far as we are justified
in challenging the doctrine, advocated by Ward and Stout, of given, fixed
extensities.   Cf. above, pp. 50, 104.

between colours and tastes, are intractable. They have to be accepted as initially given, and cannot be modified by any perceptual schema. Extensive magnitudes, on the other hand, are so to speak *drenched* with meaning. It enters into their very marrow, magically determining them to this or that standard. They are not ' given,' like qualities, but arrived at as a consequence of complexly conditioned psychical processes.

Mr. Randle states his position yet more explicitly, and in a very suggestive manner, in further defining what he entitles " sensible appearance." If by sense-datum we mean that which we immediately experience in consequence of the fact that a particular stimulus is acting on a sense-organ, then we find in the apprehension of magnitude—Mr. Randle extends this view to the apprehension of ' qualities '—that it is discoverable only as a varying function of the total field perceived, *i.e.* as ' sensible appearance.' As thus, " a *fluid* product of an elaborately constructive schematism of perception," it is in every respect the reverse of the alleged sense-datum. It is indeed immediately experienced, but only in the varying modes to which it is thus determined.

" The outstanding feature of the sensible appearance is its plasticity and fluidity, as contrasted with the stubborn and superficial rigidity of the alleged sense-datum. Its boundary lines are not fixed, and there is always more in it than ' meets the eye.' In view of the infinitely complex cross-currents of meaning that carry and constitute it, the so-called image, however determinate and ' given ' it may be at the moment of its appearance in consciousness (and it always *seems* to be a given and determinate thing), nevertheless has more of expression than of impression in it; and its possibilities as expressive of the real nature of things, are not subject to the limitations which the supposed impression (or sense-datum) seems to carry with it." [1]

There is also a second difference.

" The sense-datum is supposed to *precede* a meaning which it subsequently acquires; whereas the sensible appearance is inseparable from and *preconditioned* by the meaning which it expresses. . . . It seems to me that, logically and psychologically, meaning is the presupposition and condition precedent of every sensible appearance; sensible appearances being never impressional, but always expressional, in nature." [2]

If sense-data are regarded, in the usual manner, as so many fixed impressions, the mind will be limited merely to the combining and disjoining of them; and the continuity of the real world, as actually given in perception, will never be accounted for.

" It is not wonderful that behaviourist psychology should attempt to ignore consciousness, as not having any functional significance in the thought-process, seeing that traditional psychology has confined consciousness to *simulacra*, which by their immobility and detachment are debarred from playing any rôle in the moving drama of experience—being, like Berkeley's ideas, ' visibly inactive.' " [3]

When these statements are carried over from our apprehension of such features as extensity and motion to our apprehension of the secondary qualities, I should be inclined, as above indicated,[4] to dissent from them in certain respects. I have no inclination to defend the view of sense-data as ' raw ' and ' refractory ' material,[5] but I should hesitate to assert that the mind is " formative of its own materials," [6] or to say that " sensible appearances are the language in which the

---

[1] Randle, *loc. cit.* p. 304. [2] Randle, *loc. cit.* pp. 304-5.
[3] Randle, *loc. cit.* p. 306. [4] Pp. 77-8.
[5] Randle, *loc. cit.* p. 303. [6] Randle, *ibid.*

poetic faculty of mind tries to find, under limitations, an expression, not altogether inadequate, for those meanings which we call physical facts." [1]   I can, however, whole-heartedly agree that " experience is not connected through ' ideas,' and on the surface, but in the depth through meanings, and [that] to confine it to superficial impressions—sense-data—is necessarily to disintegrate it." [2]

[1] *Loc. cit.* p. 305.   [2] *Ibid.*

CHAPTER VII

THE CATEGORIES

BEFORE proceeding to a detailed treatment of the distinction between sense and intuition, we must come to a decision upon certain connected questions. Are time and space the only non-sensuous elements in sense-experience? Or are forms of relation, those which are usually entitled the categories, likewise demanded? Should the latter question have to be answered in the affirmative, what are the functions which fall to these categories? Are they simply *additional* to time and space, and apprehended only in certain other types of existence, such as the substantial and the causal, or are they not rather necessary for the very apprehension of time and space themselves? Also, if these categories be non-sensuously known, how come we to apprehend them?

(i.) THE SUBJECTIVIST ACCOUNT OF THE NATURE AND FUNCTIONS OF THE CATEGORIES

These questions bring into view another main tenet of the subjectivist position: namely, that our modes of apprehending outward Nature are subjectively determined, and that when we seem to ourselves in outer experience to be apprehending more than the bare sensa are qualified to reveal, we are, all unconsciously to ourselves, interpreting the sensa in the light of concepts which, however seemingly impersonal, are anthropomorphic in character, and originate from within.[1] The sensationalist starting-point[2] renders unavoidable some such conclusion. Inner experience must be made to yield richer content in proportion as outer experience fails us in this or that regard. *Conjectures* as to what supplements experience may be denied; but when experience in its actuality is alone in question, it cannot by any alchemy of logic be reduced to less than itself. What is taken from one of its two divisions must be transferred to the other, though what is thus transferred may indeed become mirage-like in the process. If Nature be in retreat, the mind must occupy, as best it can, the vacated territory; and if at last, after progressive elimination of this and that factor, only the sensa are allowed as coming to us from without, all else in Nature will have to be viewed as subjectively generated—our data for apprehending these other factors, and the specific modes in which they are apprehended, being due to the self.

This is the subjectivist doctrine of an inner and an outer path to knowledge. Through the outer path,

---

[1] The subjectivist tendencies which continue into, and so greatly pervert, Kant's teaching are, it may be noted, one and all bound up with his conviction that the categories are of subjective origin. Cf. below, p. 131.

[2] In Locke and in Berkeley, rational concepts incompatible with sensationalist principles, and yet not established in such independent manner as to justify their employment, intervene to modify their view of the situation. Descartes, on the other hand, goes so far in rejecting all aid from sensation that he has to deal with the opposite type of difficulty, viz. that of assigning to the sensa any genuinely cognitive function. *Sense*-experience is rendered unintelligible, and purely conceptual knowledge, explained as originating entirely from within, is substituted in its place. Cf. above, pp. 30-32.

that is, through sensation, we learn of the sensibly extended, the constituents of which, as capable of motion and change, are likewise in time.[1] Through the inner path, that is, through immediate consciousness, in feeling and conation, of the self as an abiding and active agent, we reflectively form the concepts of substance, causality and the like, and then, proceeding by analogy to apply them in interpretation of our outer experiences, we come to apprehend what we never directly experience, natural existences, independently real, and in causal interaction. While subjectivist thinkers may vary from one another, this is the standard-position in and about which they oscillate. They may at times show some appreciation of its unsatisfactoriness, and may seek to modify it in this or that respect, but so long as in any degree they hold to a subjectivist standpoint, they cannot succeed in breaking away from it. Those factors which, unlike space and time, cannot be smuggled into the data yielded by the senses, and which yet are admittedly involved in what we at least *appear* to experience, must perforce be obtained by the inner path.

The initial likelihood of the subjectivist line of approach goes far to justify the persistent efforts which have been made in its support, and explains why, until it had been definitely shown by Hume to be an *impasse*, the alternative position, first suggested by Kant—that the categories are essentially *objective* and are discovered through *outer* experience—should have been so universally overlooked. For is it not indeed undeniable that our inner experiences enter into our

[1] The distinction of paths breaks down, however, in regard to time : time is apprehended by the inner as well as by the outer path.

apprehensions of outer things? When two bodies clash violently, there is a sympathetic and painful reverberation in ourselves; and in less intense, but in no less obvious a manner, we congenially participate in the flight of birds, the movement of waves, the upward push of the arch in a building, and the stead-fast bearing of the supporting pillars. We do not feel ourselves to be outsiders in an alien world, but participate, together with all other natural existences, in a common life. To such an extent is this carried by the savage and by the child, that practically all the terms which they employ, and which are still in use, in describing the behaviour and energising of outer things, have in their origin been expressive of inner experiences. Even terms derived from outer happen-ings have been reinterpreted on the analogy of human activity. Motion, for example, that most universal of all outer experiences, has been interpreted as some-thing that comes into existence, exhausts itself in exercise, and ceases to be. Galileo's discovery, not made until the seventeenth century, that the analogy is totally inapplicable, and that motion (dynamically [1] conceived) is as ingenerable and as indestructible as matter itself, was undoubtedly one of the main causes which brought about the Cartesian dualism—motion being interpreted as a mode of extension, and therefore as opposite to mind.

But this recognition of the influence of inner ex-perience upon our interpretation of outer happenings must be balanced by equal recognition of the influences which act in the opposite direction. As Mr. Alexander

---

[1] *I.e.* in distinction from the merely geometrical manner in which it is also conceived by Descartes. Cf. my *Studies in the Cartesian Philosophy*, pp. 70, 75 ff.

very justly points out,[1] the influence is reciprocal, especially in the higher mental reaches. It is in and through experiencing this or that activity or type of permanence in ourselves (*i.e.* enjoying it) that we find it exemplified in the external events and things which we contemplate. We then speak of physical causality and physical substance.

" And having these conceptions we come back to our own minds and ask whether we ourselves are not subject to physical causation, or are not substances in the same sense as external things, and we may thus raise problems which seem to us of great difficulty."

It is mainly, however, to Mr. Alexander's further point that I desire to draw attention, namely, that:

" Out of this interplay of minds and things it follows that while, on the one hand, we speak of force or power in physical things in language borrowed from our own wills; on the other hand, psychological terminology, as in such terms as apprehension or comprehension or conception, is largely derived from experience of physical things or of the action of our bodies on physical things."

This, as I take it, is evidence that though at the start man exaggerates his kinship with Nature, and ascribes to her, in naïve fashion, his own experiences, yet at the same time, and for the same reason, he is *so outward-looking* that he allows Nature to colour and influence, in a quite undue degree, his appreciation and understanding of his own most characteristic activities. For, be it noted, it is not any *knowledge* of himself, not any introspective or reflective observation of the nature of the self, that yields the terms whereby natural existences are interpreted. The

[1] *Space, Time and Deity,* vol. i. pp. 187-8.

factors which intervene in his apprehension of physical happenings are feelings and conations. So outward-looking is he, that he does not reflect upon them as being inner, or as being in any peculiar sense his own. Does he not experience them when he observes two outside existences interacting, and quite as directly, though not so intensely, as when the activity is that of his own body? These feelings and conations are thus, more or less, in the position of sensa; in terms of them he experiences *all* activity, alike in himself and in others. And the outcome, as I have already said, is that while Nature is thereby brought nearer to him, he is in equal degree cut off from observation of what is most truly characteristic in his own inner life. So far as *knowledge* is concerned, it is therefore, on the whole, truer to say that the unsophisticated mind conceives the mode of the self's existence on the analogy of what material bodies are experienced to be than that bodies are conceived on the analogy of the self. Even when primitive man comes to distinguish an ' *anima* ' or ' inner ' self, what he crudely pictures is not the soul in any Platonic or psychological sense, but a mere duplicate of the body, released, indeed, from some of the limitations, chiefly of movement, to which the body is subject, but otherwise in all respects slavishly modelled upon the physical pattern.

Now if the factors directly enjoyed are feelings and conations, and if they are experienced when *any* activity is observed, whether in objects or in the self, what grounds are there for the view that the concept of substance as representing the factor of permanence, and the concept of causality as representing the factor of activity and agency, are first apprehended only in reference to the self, and are then, by analogy, imputed to other existences? If we grant the subjectivist thesis that, as data for determining the nature of independent existences, only sensa can be experienced, this view of the origin of these two concepts will doubtless, for lack of any conceivable alternative, have to be adopted. Sensa, which as such are alleged to be merely private, purely subjective, and constantly changing, could certainly never suggest them. But this surely is to prove overmuch. For if such be the character of our outer experiences, what clues can they afford sufficient to justify us in imputing to them the categories, even if otherwise obtained? If the sensa be in unceasing change, what ground is there for asserting that they represent something substantial and abiding? If they be mind-dependent, what ground is there for asserting that they causally determine one another or stand for objects which so behave? The categories, even if true of the self, will be palpable fictions when thus applied—as Hume, agreeing in these premisses, has so conclusively demonstrated.

Hume's own difficulties one and all begin when he professes to explain how these concepts, even if they be viewed as fictions, are to be accounted for, *i.e.* how we come falsely to believe that we possess ideas which really we do not possess. In denying the possibility of any direct apprehension of permanence and continuity in the world of outer experience, he has already committed himself to the denial of any kind of inner experience which will account for their apprehension, either as genuine or as fictions.

K

(ii.) A Realist View of the Nature and Functions of the Categories

It is at this point that Kant, while in the main holding to Hume's negative conclusions, reinforces and supplements them by certain others of a more positive character. In the first place, Kant shows that our apprehension of an abiding, outer world is not dependent upon the employment of concepts antecedently obtained through reflection upon the self. When we are aware, as we undoubtedly are, of permanence and continuity in the self, this can only be because we are at the same time conscious of permanence and continuity in the objects apprehended. There are not two separate paths by which, at different moments and in successive stages, separate portions of our knowledge have been acquired. Only in the process of apprehending an abiding world in outer space can there be any awareness either of the sensa or of the self. Only as elements within a total reality which includes and determines them, can either of these latter factors be discriminated and identified.[1]

---

[1] Even as regards our apprehension of other selves we are, it would seem, justified in holding that it is acquired by direct experience and not merely as an inference by analogy from the outward behaviour of other persons' bodies. The problem is, however, very complicated and difficult. The most satisfactory solution yet offered is, I believe, that given by Mr. Alexander. He points out that inference by analogy from the behaviour of other persons' bodies cannot be employed to explain the quite instinctive behaviour of animals towards each other, and also would be flatly at variance with the history of our own minds. " [The subjectivist theory] implies that we begin with a knowledge of ourselves and construe foreign selves in that likeness. Now it is almost a commonplace that the reverse is rather the case, that our reflective consciousness of ourselves arises in and through our consciousness of others. We are led, not of course to the enjoyment of ourselves but to noticing ourselves, through intercourse with others: the knowledge of ourselves and that of others grow up together. Our own

In the second place, Kant propounds a thesis, no less important and certainly not less fundamental, that the categories of substance and causality, and indeed all *a priori* categories, are essentially *objective* concepts, *i.e.* are concepts of features *constitutive of what is appre-hended*.   Kant, it is true, likewise holds, at least in his more usual modes of expressing himself, that these categories originate ' from within.'   This, however, is largely a mere prejudice, surviving from early Leib-nizian upbringing, and a main source of what is most confusing and least satisfactory in the development and formulation of his Critical teaching.   The above thesis connects with all that is most original and still vital in his theory of knowledge.

The indebtedness which Mr. Alexander, though the protagonist of so contrary a type of philosophy, acknowledges to Kant's teaching is precisely for this doctrine.

" . . . Kant is far removed from the notion that we manu-facture or work up objects of knowledge by means of the categories, still less that we impute these forms to objects. They are for him veritable elements in objective knowledge. . . . I am making these remarks not in order to fortify myself by his authority, which I certainly could not invoke, but to record a grateful conviction that with or after Plato there is nothing comparable in importance upon this subject with what may be learned from him, even by one who believes that mind which is Kant's source of categories . . . is only a name for minds which are empirical things like other empirical things.

---

individuality stands out for us against a background of other persons." To maintain such a view we must, however, be able to specify the direct experience which thus assures us not inferentially but directly of other minds.   This Mr. Alexander claims to have done in the sequel to the above quotation.   (Cf. *Space, Time and Deity,* vol. ii. pp. 31-7.)   On the general problem, cf. also Laird, *Problems of the Self,* pp. 24-8.

. . . It is to be remembered that for a man of Kant's age the only method open to a philosopher, whether it was Kant or Reid, of indicating that the world of experience contains pervasive features as well as variable ones, was to refer this part of experience to mind in its objective character." [1]

In treating of the categories, and of the part which they play in our knowledge, there are three main points upon which I shall dwell; and I may at starting indicate these in preliminary fashion.

In the first place, though consciousness or awareness, as *knowledge*, cannot be creative of its object, and must in its essential nature be *contemplative*, it is never merely contemplative, everything being done, so to speak, by the *self*-revelation of the object. This has already been indicated in the analysis of the complex processes involved in the apparently simple and direct apprehension of time and space.[2] To these processes I have, following Kant, given the title intuition. I do not, however, thereby mean to maintain what Kant teaches in the earlier portions of the *Critique of Pure Reason*, that the process of intuition is ultimate and simple, taking place, so to speak, in and by itself, in independence of all categorial thinking.[3] As I shall endeavour to show, in development of what has already been suggested, the intuitive apprehension of time and space involves the apprehension of meanings, and as factors indispensable to the possibility of such meanings, certain categorial relations.

Secondly, there are four, and only four, possible modes of existence which we can contemplate directly

---

[1] *Space, Time and Deity*, vol. i. pp. 190-2.

[2] Cf. above, p. 80 ff.

[3] This is one of the points in which Kant's ultimate results run directly counter to his initial statements.

face to face:[1] sizes, shapes, motions, and the sensa in terms of which alone any of the first three are intuitively apprehensible. As we have already noted, the sensa would seem to stand by themselves. For their apprehension we have to postulate a process of awareness, which we may entitle sensing. The first three types, on the other hand, involve much more than sensing; they involve intuition. Among the questions which we shall have to consider is the question as to how these processes, sensing and intuiting, are at once distinguished from, and related to, one another.

Thirdly, though the categories would at first sight appear to be of two distinct types, those which so directly connect with what is intuited, that they may be said to be themselves intuitable, such as the category of whole and part, and those which are apprehensible only in thought, such as the categories of substance and causality, this distinction, on further analysis, turns out to be untenable. All the categories alike involve the thought of a something—a whole, a sub- stance, or an agency—which, while it can be *located* at this and at that moment, here and there, cannot itself be intuitively apprehended. In other words, a feature common to all the categories is that they are formal and problematic in character: that to which they refer can, by their means, be entertained in thought, but cannot be rendered specific save in pro- portion as empirical data are forthcoming. Only in so far as the character of the data varies for this and that type of category, is there justification (more seeming, however, than genuine) for the distinction just suggested.

---

[1] Cf. Stout, *Manual*, p. 18 ff., and below, pp. 162-3, 166.

(a) *The Categories as involved in the Apprehension of Time and Space*

So much in general introduction: let us now consider whether and in what manner categories are involved in the apprehension of time and space. I shall do so without any attempt at exhaustive treatment. It will suffice if I can show the kind of rôle which categories play in all intuitive apprehension.

There are, it would seem, at least two categories which are indispensable for any kind of intuition, whether of time or of space—the categories of totality (whole and part) and necessitation (determining ground and conditioned consequent). To take the former first: if we conceive any specific time or specific space as always forming part of a larger time or space which conditions it, the concept of totality is obviously involved. Part is a term correlative to the term whole; to employ the former is to introduce the latter. This concept of whole and part cannot, however, be empirically, i.e. *sensuously*, acquired, if, as I have argued, the apprehensions of time and space, which presuppose it, themselves condition all empirical awareness. Nor can it be a derivative concept, elaborated out of the *intuitive* contemplation of the temporal and the spatial. The objects of intuition, time and space, are indeed apprehended as continuous; but, as we find upon analysis, such continuity already involves the employment of the category as a condition of its apprehension. For only as we employ the concept of whole and part can we apprehend specific times and specific spaces as being continuous, *i.e.* as always being wholes, relatively to their constituent parts, and

yet at the same time as always being themselves parts
of a time and space which transcend them.   If there
be no apprehension of the relation of whole and part,
there can be no apprehension of continuity.

It may, however, be objected that the continuity
which involves such concepts for its apprehension is
reached only at a late stage in mental development,
and is fundamentally different from, though elaborated
in the light of, earlier and cruder experiences of time
and space.   These latter, it will be said, yield an
experience of ' uninterruptedness ' which is unique in
kind according as it is temporal or spatial, and which
is apprehended in a purely intuitional manner, independently of all concepts which, as such, must be
later products, dependent upon the development of
discursive thinking.   But, as I have already argued,[1]
sensing and intuiting do not by themselves suffice for
the apprehension of either type of uninterruptedness.
Categorial thinking is likewise involved.   When we
apprehend that which is now actually before us as
a durational time-span or as an extended space, we
must apprehend any portion thereof as part of the
whole, and the field as a whole as itself being part
of a yet larger whole which is not itself actually
intuited.   This is necessary if either type of continuity
is to be apprehended at all.   If so much be not
granted as apprehended from the start, there is no
way of explaining how any further knowledge, ' discursive ' in type, could be acquired.   To maintain that
thought must in all cases be subsequent to intuition
would therefore seem to be impossible.   That would
rule out those very experiences which, by admission,
are necessary to the formation, at a later stage, of the

[1] Cf. above, pp. 132, 134.

appropriate concepts. Initially, the presupposed categorial concepts must, indeed, be employed without
explicit formulation, much in the manner in which
a child employs the category of causality when it
assumes that the fire which has burnt it once will,
if approached too closely, burn it again. For as
Mr. Stout, in treating of such early stages of mental
development in his *Manual of Psychology*,[1] so consistently argues, categories first reveal their presence in
a practical manner as determining behaviour. Consciousness, under their guidance, reaches out and
anticipates a wider or future experience. Mr. Stout,
as we have noted,[2] himself assumes a category of
"spatial unity"; but as I have sought to show, such
a category would seem to be too general in character
to serve the purposes for which it is postulated; and
in any case is surely more correctly defined as being
the category of whole and part applied to, or rather
essentially and inseparably involved in, the apprehension of each and every extension. These same
remarks will equally apply to Mr. Stout's category of
" temporal unity."

To repeat, apprehension of continuity in all its
spatial and temporal modes presupposes the employment of the category of whole and part, and cannot
therefore account for our first apprehension of it.
Though as a relational category it is not, in and by
itself, intuitable, yet as employed in all intuitive apprehension it makes possible our apprehension of that
general or universal meaning which finds such inexhaustibly manifold embodiment in the times and
spaces which, thanks to its aid, we do actually intuite
in the concrete. In continuity, as intuitively appre-

----

[1] Cf. p. 436 ff.   [2] Above, p. 110 ff.

hended in the forms of time and space, the problem of
the one and the many, of the universal and the particular, of meaning and that which embodies meaning,
presents itself in its most fundamental form. The
manyness of time or of space is only apprehensible in
terms of the oneness of each; and yet any given
example of this oneness, as found in a given space or
a given time, is itself, relatively to its constituent parts,
only apprehensible in the same way. What Whitehead calls ' extensity,' that is, the property of extending
one over the other, is a universal characteristic of
all times and of all spaces; and as universal, it involves
a meaning in which the categorial relation is an essential
element.

A similar argument can be stated in terms of the
connected category of necessitation—the concept common to logical ground and causal connection. This
category also, it would seem, is involved in the
apprehension of the kind of continuity exemplified
by both time and space. Any particular time or any
particular space, however large or however small, is
conditioned and made possible by the earlier time and
by the wider space which leads into or contains it.
That is to say, the kind of wholeness which is to be
found in time and space is one that determines the
elements constituent of it. Though the category may
therefore be said to express a feature quite fundamental
to both time and space, and actually constituent of
them, none the less this feature, in order to be
intuited, must be apprehended, not merely in the
particularity of some one actual instance, but again
as a universal meaning in which the categorial relation
is involved.

Though the fact that the category of necessitation,

while it is distinct from that of totality,[1] is yet required in apprehending the relation by which a whole is a whole relatively to its parts, may not be very evident, or may even be questionable in the case of more concrete wholes, it is easily discernible in regard to temporal and spatial wholes, taken in their temporal and spatial aspects. The ' now ' cannot come to exist save in and through the ' no longer ' ; the triangle which we describe in marking off a space by the intersection of three straight lines cannot exist save in and through the wider space within which it lies; and neither type of existence can, it would seem, be apprehended save as thus determined in a wider context.

In general, then, we can say that the primary function of such categories as the above is not to clarify our intuitions, but to make them possible. The relations in question can, indeed, be discovered by the processes of analytic thinking, as actually constituent of what is intuited. But they are universals, and thus are not themselves intuited. Since, then, one constituent of the intuited is apprehended by thought, categorial thinking is a condition of, and is not derived from, intuition.

Time and space being, as they are, complex, it is not surprising that our intuition of them should thus rest on a variety of conditions. And since time and space are uniform as well as complex—uniformity is only another name for their continuity—and are apprehended as thus uniform, what other agency than the entertaining of *universal* meanings, made possible by categorial thinking, can be really adequate to the needs of the situation?

In one important respect time and space are appre-

---

[1] Cf. the passage quoted from Mr. Alexander, below, p. 142 *n.*

hended in a manner analogous to the categorial relations; namely, as always extending beyond the sensuously intuited, and yet as presupposed in it.   In mature
and explicit consciousness, and, as we may therefore
argue, also in implicit consciousness, the thought or
conception of time and space, in their ' totality,' is a
condition of the apprehension of either in any given
sensuous experience; the thought of something not
sensuously given conditions the sensuous experiences
which are given.   And while what is thus thought as
transcending the given is a continuation of what is
apprehended in the given, it is not first generated by
prolongation of the given.   On the contrary, the given
is apprehensible only as sequent upon, or as delimited
from, the not - given.   This, *mutatis mutandis*, is
analogous to the manner in which we apprehend the
categorial relations.   They have a meaning wider
and more general than that which is to be found in
any one of the primary experiences in which they
come to consciousness.   Indeed, in the case of the
category of totality, there is a conflict between the
very nature of the time and space ' forms ' which
embody it, and the demands of the category itself—
a conflict which constrains the mind to the drawing
of the fundamental distinction between the actual and
the illusory, between reality and appearance.[1]

The concepts of continuity, infinitude, and absoluteness are, it would seem, derivative concepts, partly
conceptual and partly intuitional in character.   To
the concept of continuity I have already referred.   In
it the categories of totality and necessitation are
employed to make possible the intuitive experience of
time and space.   The extended in time and space is

[1] Cf. below, pp. 140-43, 235-6.

always manifold, and indeed inexhaustibly manifold; and yet never fails to preserve its aspect of being, relatively to its constituent parts, a genuine totality. We cannot ignore either aspect; and we contrive to combine them in the apprehension of time and space as continuous. In continuity the whole is so determinant of its constituent parts that it maintains itself as continuous, however far analysis be carried; that is, it cannot be conceived as an aggregate, built up of parts which it does not itself make possible.

This concept of continuity, in turn, is found to lead up to, and to involve, the concept of infinity in time and space. Time and space, being apprehended as continuous, must also be apprehended as infinite. For if they be continuous, then however small or however large a given time or space may be, the same truth holds, namely that they continue, and are continued into, a time and a space which transcend them.

The concept of absoluteness is of kindred character. If everything experienced is experienced as belonging to a time-space world, nothing, it would seem, can be apprehended by us save as belonging to, and forming part of, a whole more comprehensive than itself, *i.e.* as conditioned or non-absolute. Owing to this fundamental characteristic of our experience we possess a criterion whereby we are enabled to distinguish between truth and falsity, between appearance and reality. What can be apprehended as fitting into the whole of our experience, however wide, is true and real; what cannot be so interpreted is false and illusory.

But this criterion we are constrained to apply to the entire time-space world; and when we do so, a conflict arises between the aspect of time and space which gains expression through the category of totality and that other connected aspect which is more appropriately expressed through the category of necessitation. There are two, and, as it would seem, only two alternatives. Either we rest in the conception of the actual infinite, and all possibility of absoluteness, *i.e.* of a totality which is not itself subordinated within a wider whole, is ruled out. Or, on the other hand, we find in experience some justification for believing that the infinitude of Euclidean time and space does not hold of reality, properly understood.

For this latter attitude we may claim justification on the ground that certain dominant and decisive experiences disclose to us, through their spiritual significance, types of reality not compatible with the uniformity of the actual infinite; or else through mathematico-physical science we may achieve, in terms of a non-Euclidean time-space system, a genuine realisation of wholeness and unity. Ultimately these two lines of argument may prove to be not incompatible. For there is no apparent reason why the two methods may not be combined. In either case— though not on the view of reality as actually infinite —the distinction between empirical reality and empirical illusion can then be extended, so as to yield the wider-reaching distinction between appearance and reality—appearance being conceived as that which, if it could be apprehended (as it cannot, so long as appearance is appearance) in the complete context to which it ultimately belongs, would be otherwise apprehended than it is actually apprehended. We shall not thereby be committed to the view that nothing can be known by us save as appearance, and that genuine reality is in all spheres closed to our view. But it will allow of our holding, should evidence to this effect be forthcoming, that at least in certain cases what we are apt to view as genuine reality is but appearance. Though the distinction is itself a metaphysical one, the extent and consequences of its application can, like that between empirical reality and empirical illusion, be determined only by empirical investigation. It will alter, widen, or narrow, as experience matures, and according as the results of experience point to a close-knit or to an opener type of wholeness in the absolutely real.[1]

Thus, on this view, no additional semi-mystical *a priori* concepts, such as the ' Absolute ' or the ' Unconditioned ' require to be postulated. What Kant entitles the ' Ideas of Reason ' are simply special applications of the category of totality to empirically acquired material. Nothing, not even time or space, can be apprehended by us save in conformity with

[1] Mr. Alexander, in criticising the view, as held by Mr. Bosanquet, that the only satisfactory statement of a cause is the whole universe, proceeds : " If this were true the idea of cause would indeed retain a certain usefulness in practice, but as a theoretical basis of procedure in science it would be useless. But the objection rests on a misconception. It assumes that the operation of the stars is a motion which interferes with the causal act by which a man knocks another down; and does so because there is direct or indirect connection between all parts of the universe, throughout Space-Time. The question rather is whether the intimate causal relation mentioned is interfered with by the rest of the universe which undoubtedly sustains it. . . . What science has to do is just to discover these limited, intimate, relations of existents which are called causal ones. Everything which it finds by inquiry relevant has to be included and becomes part of the substances involved. Everything which, though its presence is assumed, does not interfere so as to control or vitiate, lapses for the special causal relation into the position of an immaterial condition" (*Space, Time and Deity*, vol. i. pp. 289-90). Cf. also Broad, *Perception, Physics and Reality*, pp. 143-6.

what this category prescribes; and, in fateful consequence of this fundamental characteristic, the human mind, in all its activities, is essentially metaphysical, always apprehending what is experienced as implying more than it is ever itself experienced as being. Our consciousness is self-transcending and self-limiting, viewing the intuited in terms of the non-intuited, the parts in terms of a conditioning whole. And so we are tied down to two alternatives, either the actual infinite or an ultimate whole, *i.e.* a whole which is not itself part of a more comprehensive whole. Only on the latter alternative will there exist what is properly describable as an Absolute or Unconditioned. For the notion of a whole which does not itself fall within a wider whole is just the notion of the Unconditioned—that which has no conditions which determine it from without. And this conception is possible, even though we are not able to say what such a whole can be.

On the other alternative—the real being actually infinite, and therefore not allowing of totality, save in the modified form of continuity—Absoluteness and Unconditionedness are meaningless and self-contradictory concepts. The ideal which has inspired so many intellectual inquiries, that of bringing within the scope of a single system all the factors which are determinant of existences apprehended in sense-experience, will then have to be viewed as an ideal which not only is not attainable, but which, when conceived as representing ultimate reality, just thereby *mis*represents it.

(b) The Formal Problematic Character of the Categories

Owing to the manner in which the various categories are bound up with the category of totality, a further conclusion seems to follow, namely, that they share in its problematic character, enabling us to think and locate, but never to comprehend (in the sense of defining in a positive manner) that to which they refer.   Such positive knowledge of the nature of the unity apprehended must in all cases be obtained, when it is obtainable, from empirical data.   If these assertions be true, they are highly important; and I shall therefore dwell upon them at some length.

That the category of totality is not inappropriately describable as an essentially problematic conception, is a statement which rests upon the following grounds. No one can deny that we know quite definitely what is meant by temporal and spatial inclusion.   The ' specious present' includes within itself the times covered by each of its constituent events; a yard includes the distances represented by each of its constituent feet.[1]   Such relations of inclusion are intuitively

---

[1] Cf. Whitehead, *The Concept of Nature*, pp. 58-9: " Durations can have the two-termed relational property of extending one over the other.   Thus the duration which is all nature during a certain minute extends over the duration which is all nature during the thirtieth second of that minute. This relation of ' extending over '—' extension,' as I shall call it—is a fundamental natural relation whose field comprises more than durations. . . . I shall . . . maintain that the same relation of extension lies at the base both of temporal and spatial extension. . . . I shall use the terms ' whole ' and ' part ' exclusively in this sense, that the ' part ' is an event which is extended over by the other event which is the ' whole.'   Thus in my nomenclature ' whole ' and ' part ' refer exclusively to this fundamental relation of extension. . . . The continuity of nature arises from extension. . . . Accordingly there are no maximum durations and no minimum durations.   Thus there is no atomic structure of durations,

apprehended in the time-span of durational consciousness and in the direct apprehension of the given
spatial field; and by reasoning therefrom we can
in thought give a quite precise meaning to similar
relations on the larger scales that exceed immediate
experience. Thus if by 'totality' we mean simply
that which stands to its constituents in the relation of
a temporal or spatial whole, immediate experience
suffices to yield to the category a meaning so definite
that we can never be in doubt what we should mean
thereby, or to what types of existences it is applicable.
Also, we are able, by means of concepts which have
been elaborated by the mathematician, to define this
relation in strictly conceptual terms. The parts are
never truly isolable; they pass continuously into one
another, like the positive real numbers, which do not
start with the number 1, and proceed by jerks through
the successive integers, but proceed from o continuously through the infinitely numerous intermediate
numbers into 1, and through 1 similarly into 2, and
so forth. To use the prescribed technical terms, they
constitute a 'compact series,' such that between any two
constituents another constituent of the same order has
always to be conceived as intervening. Just as there
are never two 'next' real numbers, so there are never
two 'next' points either in time or in space.

Thus in conceptually describing the relation of
inclusion (or uninterruptedness) which we apprehend
intuitively, we find ourselves constrained to employ
the concept of continuity; and as we further find, the

---

and the perfect definition of a duration, so as to mark out its individuality
and distinguish it from highly analogous durations over which it is passing,
or which are passing over it, is an arbitrary postulate of thought. . . .
Exactness is an ideal of thought, and is only realised in experience by the
selection of a route of approximation." Cf. below, p. 147 *n.*

concept of whole and part is definite and precise only in proportion as that of continuity is so likewise.

What, however, is it that the latter concept achieves in this regard? May we not say that what it does is to define the *relations* in which parts that are to be parts of temporal or spatial wholes must stand to one another, and that this is its sole function? It does not profess to assign to the term ' totality ' or ' wholeness ' or ' inclusion ' any meaning which is not equally appropriate to the parts composing it. For the continuity which it prescribes to parts that are to be parts is a continuity which for the same reason must belong to the whole within which they fall. It too must be a part to a larger whole, just as are its parts to it. It is a whole only in the sense in which some particular number is a whole, namely, that, as being a number which we have found reason to select from a series of numbers; it is a total with reference to its constituent units, but is itself a constituent of all higher numbers.[1] This is not a wholeness which in any adequate fashion meets the demands of the concept which we employ in its apprehension.

This last statement calls for further justification. While the concepts of whole and of part are, we may say, the *relata* which we think in thinking the *relations* constituent of continuity, the description above given of continuity defines only the relations and not the relata themselves. It tells us in what relations ' parts ' must stand to other parts if a whole is to exist. It does, indeed, define each part by its position in the

---

[1] The account here given of ' wholeness ' connects with that given of infinitude. Any infinite magnitude is a part of an infinite magnitude, and has an infinite magnitude as a part. The above method of defining ' wholeness ' thus involves all the problems of continuity and therefore of the actual infinite.

series; but this position, in turn, is itself defined only through the relations in which it stands to other positions similarly defined.   That which in parts makes them capable of constituting a whole is not explained, but from start to finish presupposed.   So also with the correlative relatum, that of wholeness. It too is defined only by the relations in which it stands to its own constituents.   Either it is that which is given, and to which analysis, following the method of 'extensive abstraction,'[1] can be applied; or it is constructed through synthesis of parts of the same nature as itself, in which case it is reached by reversing the process whereby we advance to the constituent elements.   In either case, so far is it from having any kind of wholeness which prevents it from being in equal degree partial, that, on the contrary, what renders it a whole, namely, its essential continuity, is likewise what prevents it from ever itself being anything save a part in a still larger whole of the same type.   While, therefore, the category of totality enables us to apprehend the *relation* of inclusion, it does not, in its temporal and spatial, any more than in its numerical employment, thereby enable us to discern any existence which adequately embodies the meaning to which it gives expression; and this, it would seem, is why it has to voice itself in further demands which the sciences and metaphysics arise in order to satisfy.

But what, it may be asked, is the meaning to which the category gives expression, if it be not a meaning which is adequately apprehended in temporal and

[1] Cf. Whitehead, *The Concept of Nature*, pp. 78-9 : " The clue discovered by the commonsense of mankind and systematically utilised in science is what I have elsewhere called the law of convergence to simplicity by diminution of extent." Cf. p. 57 : "A moment is a limit to which we approach as we confine attention to durations of minimum extension."

spatial 'wholes.' I have already stated that the category is problematic, enabling us to think and locate, though never to specify that to which it refers. What I thereby desire to signify is that *the category is formal*, not specific, *in character*. So far as the category, in and by itself, is our guide, *that to which it is to be applicable can be stated only in negative terms, as what is not partial or incomplete*.

This formal character belongs indeed to all the categories, and is one of their chief merits. It is illustrated even in the characters of time and space. For is not each of these, notwithstanding the uniqueness of its own positive nature, none the less astonishingly catholic in its compatibility with a quite inexhaustible variety of different types of existences and occurrences? The categories exhibit a similar flexibility, and while not allowing us to predict what precisely we shall find, guide us to regions where we may hope to make discoveries, and supply terms in which these discoveries can always be stated once they are made. Thus the category of totality, while leading us to seek alike in time and in space, and in regard to what is experienced in these media, for what will complete the incomplete, does so without enabling us to anticipate in what this completeness will be found to consist.[1]   As we have

---

[1] This is a characteristic of the categories to which Mr. Stout has frequently drawn attention. Cf. *Proc. Arist. Soc.*, 1914–15, Note on 'Knowledge by acquaintance' and 'Knowledge about,' pp. 350-51: "I take knowledge by description to be as ultimate as knowledge by acquaintance. The possibility of it rests for me on the fact that some entities, at least, have a certain kind of incompleteness, such that on apprehending them we are able to apprehend them as being incomplete and are therefore aware of something as being necessary to complete them. We may also know that the something, inasmuch as it has to satisfy this condition, must be of a certain general character. But its specific and detailed nature has, at least in most cases, to be otherwise ascertained."

already observed, in dealing with temporal and spatial
' wholes,' the specific nature of the ' wholeness '
obtained is not in either case prescribed by the category, but is differently determined according as the
medium in which it is being applied is temporal or
spatial.   Also, for its adequate conceptual definition it
demands the expert knowledge of the mathematician.
Yet even so, the notion of wholeness thus obtained
fails to measure up to what the category prescribes.
It is indeed ' wholeness '—so far we locate correctly—
relatively to its parts.   But since the very reason which
determines us to regard it as being, in this respect, a
whole, constrains us to regard it as always itself a part
in a yet larger whole of the same type, the formal
requirement of the category is not completely fulfilled.

When we pass to physical applications of the
category, the situation is different; but the same conclusion none the less follows for other reasons.   When
we employ the category in the apprehension of physical
existences in time and space, some empirical factor
enters ' from without,' imposing a limitation which
time and space, as continuous, cannot themselves yield;
and within this empirically defined time-span or space-
area totality is then located.   When, for instance, we
treat a cloud as a unity, we do so because, in contrast
to its surroundings, it moves as a single whole—this
motion being directly apprehended owing to the fact
that the cloud is more or less uniformly coloured, and
so stands out against its differently coloured background.   In all such cases as this—another example
would be a train consisting of engine and carriages—
we locate unity where we find community of motion.
Now obviously these instances are no better fitted
than are times and spaces to embody, in any adequate

fashion, the meaning which the category expresses. Owing to sharpness of outline and the consequent absence of continuity we are no longer constrained to regard each cloud as part of a yet larger cloud; but on the other hand, owing to the irregular and changeable form of the outline, and the tendency of the cloud to break up into parts, each with its own outline and motion, this advantage (if it may be so called) is more than counterbalanced. Either the object is entitled a unity only by courtesy and for convenience in the making of practical judgements, or, in proportion as it is more than this, it is of a problematic character, and for the determination of the nature and extent of the unity referred to we have to rely exclusively upon empirical data. The mere employment of the category, by itself, decides nothing.

The situation is again different when the application of the category is determined by the results of experimental investigation, as when the physicist applies the category in defining the nature of a molecule or atom or electron. The difficulties which emerge are indeed, at first sight, similar to those which suggest themselves in reference to the cloud. Each is a plurality, and the two former can be broken up into their components. But what mainly justifies the employment of the category is that each is more than merely an aggregate of its parts, and that the genuineness of its unity can be exhibited in a variety of different reactions, not merely in temporary community of visible motion or temporary persistence of visible outline. To the extent, however, to which the unity is genuine, it is certainly not predetermined by the category, and even its *general* nature can only be discovered in and through experimental investigation.

Also, as thus determined, it is found to vary greatly in type. The molecule is richer in content but less stable in structure than the atom, and the atom, in turn, than the electron; and to ask whether the molecule or the electron is the truer embodiment of unity is to raise a question which is more easily asked than answered. For it does not merely turn upon the definition of terms, but upon issues which are fundamental alike in science and in philosophy. Usually, or at least until quite recently, the physicist has conceived these ultimate entities somewhat in the manner of Kelvin's vortex-atoms, as differentiations, stresses, or the like, in some continuous medium which has the fundamental characteristics of space, and therefore yields no better embodiment for the category than does space itself.[1] Also the concept of energy, and therewith the categories of substance and causality, enter to complicate the issues.

The problematic, and strictly formal, character of the category of totality becomes still more obvious when we pass to its employment in the apprehension of the living organism and of the self. For while these two types of existence give a very strong impression of being genuine unities, the character of their unity is proportionately problematic, transcending our present means of comprehension. That the organism is in some manner or degree a genuine unity, and is at least a fuller and richer whole than any of its parts, will be agreed to by all biologists save those who adopt the so-called 'mechanistic' position in its most extreme form, and so treat the organism as being merely a collocation of purely physical entities, and

---

[1] Cf. Lord Salisbury's dictum: "By ether would appear to be meant simply the substantive of the verb to undulate."

regard each of these entities as more fittingly expressive of the concept of unity than is the organism as a whole. The ambiguity of the position is concealed by the supposed analogy of the organism to a machine. That analogy is not applicable unless the non-scientific hypothesis of special creation is used to justify the teleological conceptions apart from which the term 'machine' has no definiteness of meaning.

If, however, we allow that the living organism is a more genuine embodiment of unity than are purely physical existences, and that it has, for instance, a self-preservative tendency, such as gives rise to a 'struggle for existence,' we must also grant that, to the very extent to which this is so, our knowledge not only of its precise but even of its general nature is wholly dependent upon empirical investigation.[1] Also, owing to the manner in which, as our knowledge has gained increase, the organic processes have become for us not less but more complex, without any limit thereto being yet discernible, the nature of the living organism far transcends our present means of comprehension. No theory of 'vital control' or of 'entelechy' in the least avails to explain the type of unity which the living thing possesses. At best the vitalist position can only be formulated as being that the unity of the organism is its fundamental characteristic, and that it has to be taken into account if any complete, or ap-

---

[1] Cf. Pringle-Pattison, *The Idea of Immortality*, p. 93: "The parts of an organism are so much members one of another and of the whole which they constitute—they are so interpenetrative in their action—that it is hardly a paradox to say that the organism *qua* organism is not in space at all. Part and whole acquire here a meaning unknown to physics, a meaning in which the necessary correlation of the terms is for the first time apparent. The organism . . . is the first real whole, the first natural unity." But must it not be added that this unity is proportionately problematic?

proximately complete, explanation is to be given of the processes which, occurring within it, serve to maintain it in existence.[1]   But even so much can be asserted only if the assertion be backed by experimental evidence, and by demonstration of the precise means whereby the organism is enabled to control and direct the processes which, by admission, are necessary to uphold it.   And so in this sphere also the category of totality continues to be a strictly problematic concept, guiding us in the locating of unity and in the seeking out of the data whereby its nature may, as we trust, be progressively defined, but never, in and by itself, sufficing for its comprehension, and never, in any *positive* manner, predetermining even the general features of that which we are endeavouring to explain.

Similar remarks are in order when the category of totality is employed to define the nature of the self. That the self is in some manner and degree a unity is again beyond question, but when we seek to define the character and exact degree of this unity, problems multiply.   As I shall have occasion to maintain in later chapters, the self is conditioned in a twofold manner.   On the subjective side it consists in psychical powers and dispositions which are highly complex, and which in some manner, not precisely definable, are conditioned by vital processes in the body, and more especially in the brain.   On the objective side the self also demands for its possibility the objective field of our sense-experience; for this field is no less necessary to the possibility of conscious-

[1] This is the position maintained by Dr. J. S. Haldane in his *Organism and Environment as illustrated by the Physiology of Breathing* (New Haven, 1917).

ness than are the conscious processes themselves.[1]
Thus from both sides, the subjective and the objective,
the self has its roots and filaments inextricably inter-
woven with what lies, or seems to lie, beyond itself:
it is a self at all only because reality in *all* its other
aspects is ministrant to it.   And yet we speak of it
as a unity!   Advisedly so, but *not* because we can
profess to comprehend, even distantly, how it is
possible that it should be so.   The unity of the self
is, if anything, even less comprehensible than the
unity of the living organism—as indeed we should
expect, if, as would seem to be the case, the organism

---

[1] " That there cannot be an act of knowing without something to
know; or, more generally, that there cannot be an act of judging, even an
act of apprehending at all, without something to judge, something to
apprehend, is one of the most self-evident propositions yielded by a quite
elementary consideration of these processes." (Quoted by Mr. G. Dawes
Hicks from Meinong, *Proc. Arist. Soc.*, 1916–17, pp. 318-19.)   Mr. Dawes
Hicks adds in comment: " [Meinong] lays it down as a characteristic
feature of the psychical, in contradistinction to the non-psychical, that it
is directed upon something (*auf etwas gerichtet*), and that this ' something '
is neither identical with nor partially identical with the psychical act
directed upon it.   A mental act is not, in other words, an event which is
complete in itself.   In a sense the same is, no doubt, true of every event.
A physical event is dependent for its occurrence upon what is other than
itself.   But the dependence here in question is a dependence of a totally
different order.   A physical event can be described in and for itself.   Not
so, a mental event.   To speak of an act of awareness simply would be to
speak of that which is never met with.   Awareness in and for itself has
no existence, and, indeed, no meaning; a ' something ' of which there
is awareness is its indispensable correlative." Cf. Alexander, *Space, Time
and Deity*, vol. ii. pp. 105 and 115: " The plant selects from the soil; but
the phosphates are already there, and it does not make them.   Mind is
equally a reaction to external things and what it selects for its object is
present in the thing or in some other part of the universe.   So far is the
object from being dependent on the mind that, on the contrary, the mind is,
at any rate for its original material, dependent on the object; just as the
silver must exist before it can be used as a shilling and be impressed with
the King's effigy." " Consciousness exists in the intercourse of the conscious being and things, and is neither equivalent to the objects it selects
nor can exist without those objects."

is but one among the many conditions upon which the existence of the self depends. The self is not *self*-subsistent. If it survives the death of the body, it can do so only in so far as reality continues to uphold it by other and different means.[1]

When we pass beyond these empirical unities to such a metaphysical entity as the Universe, and ask whether we are able to define in any *positive* manner in what the totality of the Universe consists, the fact that our concept of totality is problematic requires no lengthy argument. As we have already noted,[2] the raising of this question brings us face to face with the problem of the actual infinite. In recognising continuity as a fundamental feature of reality, so far as reality is in time and space, have we committed ourselves to acceptance of the actual infinite, and therefore to denial of unity in every absolute sense? Or are there alternative possibilities? Obviously these questions cannot be answered simply through analysis of any category. The notion of the actual infinite is not inherently self-contradictory; to that extent it is a genuine possibility. In deciding what other possibilities there may be, and which best harmonise with our total experience, the mathematical sciences and the

---

[1] A passage to this effect lingers in my memory from Mr. Stout's Gifford Lectures. I cannot, however, recall it sufficiently accurately for purposes of quotation. Cf. Stout, *Some Fundamental Points in the Theory of Knowledge* (St. Andrews University Quincentenary Publications, 1911), p. 12 : " It will be seen that in treating of the unity of the self I have omitted all reference to self-consciousness. I have done so intentionally, on the ground that there can be no consciousness of self unless there is a self to be conscious of. But this, in the first instance, can only be constituted by acts which have for their objects something other than their own being. . . . Given a self to know, there is no reason why it should not be known." Cf. also Pringle-Pattison, *The Idea of Immortality*, pp. 195-7.

[2] Cf. above, pp. 140-43.

humanistic disciplines alike have the right to claim a
hearing. For in both of these diverse fields data are
procurable which have a bearing, direct or indirect,
upon the issues at stake. Though the problem is
metaphysical, it can only be decided in the light of
specific evidence, empirically acquired.

(c) The Relations holding between Sensing, Categorial Thinking, and Intuiting

We are now in a position to consider the relations
in which sensing, categorial thinking, and intuiting
stand to one another. As I have been insisting,
intuition is not purely receptive; it is the apprehension of what is contemplated, in terms of meaning
— that which is apprehended being apprehended
quite as much in and through these meanings as in
and through what is directly ' seen ' or ' touched.'
This is, indeed, the essential difference between
sensing and intuiting. In sensing a red we apprehend
an entity by direct acquaintance. We stand over
against it, and it reveals to us its actual nature. It
cannot, of course, by itself form a complete field of
consciousness. Consciousness, if limited to it, would
thereby be made to vanish. But for its apprehension,
so far as its redness is concerned, no further meaning,
demanding categorial expression, is involved. Not
so with the objects of intuition. Time and space,
whatever else they may likewise be, are relational
forms of existence. For though they can be directly
contemplated in terms of sensa, this, it would seem,
is only possible because an elaborate complexity of
categorial relations is being simultaneously apprehended, as constituting the nature of what is thus

perceived. Red, we may say, is an opaque entity; it is a *differentiating* factor in the real. Time and space, on the other hand, are, so to speak, surcharged with meaning; and while each is unique in its kind, they *integrate* with one another and with all existing things and events.

Connected therewith is a second difference, namely, that our first knowledge of red cannot be further developed. We may, of course, learn much about the physical and physiological antecedents of the redness; but in the initial experience we have something which the blind can never acquire, and which the scientist is not in the least concerned to alter or enlarge. Time and space, on the other hand, being apprehended in terms of meanings as well as of what is directly contemplated, demand for their ' adequate ' apprehension vaster labours than the mathematicians of genius from Pythagoras to Einstein have yet accomplished. Thus a distinguished mathematician can venture to describe the teaching, in regard to time, space, and matter, now most generally accepted, at least among the non - mathematical, as being benightedly mediaeval.

" There is a trimness about it, with its instantaneous present, its vanished past, its non-existent future, and its inert matter. This trimness is very mediaeval and ill accords with brute fact. The theory which I am urging admits a greater ultimate mystery and a deeper ignorance. . . . It is impossible to meditate on time and the mystery of the creative passage of nature without an overwhelming emotion at the limitations of human intelligence." [1]

[1] *The Concept of Nature*, p. 73. Cf. p. 178 on ' the creative advance of nature ': " We habitually muddle together this creative advance, which we experience and know as the perpetual transition of nature into novelty, with the single-term series which we naturally employ for measurement."

Thus categorial thinking, owing to its direct connection with intuition, connects also, indirectly, with sensing. Intuition is impossible without categorial thinking; nothing can be intuited save by the aid of meanings conceptually entertained. And since sensa can never by themselves constitute a complete presentational field, but require as supplementary factors the objects of intuition, the occurrence of sensing is likewise conditioned by categorial thinking. Complete consciousness, *i.e.* any actual consciousness, involves all three—on the objective side, the sensa, the categorial relations, time, and space; on the subjective side, sensing, categorial thinking, and intuiting.

As already noted, what is known as in time and space is always apprehended as prolonged and supplemented in and through ideal meanings. When we look out upon a visual field, the opaque interior of the objects seen, and those of their surfaces which are turned away from us, exist for us in thought, that is, in ideal construction. So much is universally recognised; but as I have endeavoured to show,[1] the ideal factor enters even into what, in seeming, is utterly immediate, viz. the discrimination of the given shapes and sizes, of the given times and motions. And though ideal meaning is thus all-pervasive, it does not render the world thereby apprehended subjective or merely imaginary. On the contrary, these meanings disclose to us, much more completely than can the sensa, the constitution and scope of the independently real.[2]

---

[1] Above, p. 134 ff.

[2] Cf. *Space, Time and Deity*, vol. i. pp. 41-2 : " We must not imagine that the elements are unreal because they are ideal constructions, as the word construction is apt to suggest, any more than we must imagine that a man's back is unreal because I do not see it but only imagine it or have it in idea. For sense has no monopoly of reality. We reach reality by all

Space is indeed visually intuitable only as it is coloured; but the factor of thought is no less necessary than the factor of sense, in order that ' spreadoutness ' be apprehensible in intuition.

Though Mr. Alexander would very justly disavow the interpretation which I shall place upon what he is saying, I cannot resist quoting the following happily expressed passage:

" . . . reality is not limited to sensible constituents but contains ideal and conceptual ones. The back of a solid object which we see in front, the taste of an orange which we feel or see are ideal, but they belong none the less to the real solid and the real orange. Likewise the concept or thought of a dog is as real a constituent of the dog as what makes him a singular thing. It is its structural plan. Like all the objects of our experience, any part of space contains the two aspects of singularity and universality. It is itself and it follows a law of structure. Points are singular, but they have such structure as becomes a point and are so far universal." [1]

If the above statements be agreed to, we shall be justified in concluding that, so far as time and space are concerned, thought and intuition *mutually* condition one another. For though continuity must be thought in order to be intuited, it is no less true that when thus thought, through the appropriate concepts, what is intuited reveals to us a type of ' uninterruptedness ' which is unique in its kind and could never have been anticipated had the categorial concepts alone been at our disposal. Space can be apprehended only because it is actually there, and in the process of intuition

---

our powers. All we have to be sure of is that we use them rightly, so that the whole, by whatever powers of ours it is apprehended, shall be itself and self-consistent."

[1] *Space, Time and Deity*, vol. i. p. 151.

presents itself to us in its own person.   The employment of certain categorial concepts is a condition
antecedent to our intuiting an existence of this
general type (*i.e.* one which possesses continuity);
but the intuition, when it comes, discloses a something
not otherwise knowable.   Intuition, we may say, is so
far like sensing in that it has the contemplative character, and gives to something objective the opportunity
for its *self*-revelation.   The knower must be adequately
equipped; but it is upon the object that the outcome
depends.

The presence in the intuited of more than can be
anticipated through the categorial concepts involved
in its apprehension is patently evident when we consider that the categorial factors are seemingly identical
for both time and space.[1]   Yet time and space, however they may agree in certain fundamental features
which concern their singleness and continuity, are
otherwise extraordinarily different.   Popular thought
may be in error when it conceives them as separate
existences.   They may, as many mathematicians maintain, condition one another; and time be, as it were,
only a dimension which with space makes up a four-
dimensional system.   Still it remains none the less
true that time is not reducible to space, if it be viewed
as different from space, nor to the other three dimensions, if it be assimilated to space, and that only in
intuition, not in conceptual thinking, can what thus
uniquely distinguishes it be disclosed to our view.

But, it will be again objected, if each type of continuity is actually embodied in the time and the space
which we intuite, and if in intuition time and space
stand *self*-revealed, will not contemplation, conceived

---

[1] Also for number.

as a process analogous to sensing, by itself suffice for their apprehension? This objection I suppose myself to have already answered in dealing with the apprehension of a durational span and an extensive field.[1] If duration cannot be passively contemplated, neither can the special type of ' uninterrupted plurality ' that constitutes time; and the same must be true of ' uninterrupted plurality ' in its spatial form. Intuition, it would seem, can remain intuitive and be genuinely contemplative, even though, for its actualisation, it be complexly conditioned on the subjective side. Here, as so universally throughout the natural world, seeming simplicity is but masked complexity, and is only possible through the co-operation of a multitude of factors which do not disclose themselves to superficial view.

Consciousness, to repeat, even when most truly contemplative, is never merely contemplative, everything being done, so to speak, by the self-revealing of the object. We may not argue that because sensing allows, or rather perhaps constrains to, this interpretation, intuiting may do so likewise. For sensing, if my general thesis be sound, is itself only possible in so far as it is supplemented by processes of a fundamentally different character. The total field of our apprehension, or at least those of its features which are pervasive of it, cannot be apprehended in the same manner as its sensory elements.

(d) The Categories of Substance and Causality

But the categories, besides thus serving, in co-operation with the intuited, to make possible our

---

[1] Above, p. 80 ff.

M

intuitions, have also a further function.   They have, as we find, a wider range, and make possible meanings —such as substance and causality—which can have no equivalent in exclusively spatial and temporal relations. Intuition has, it is true, a sponge-like quality whereby it appropriates to itself the contributions of thought; as in the analysis of sense-perception, only with diffi- culty, and not by any method of isolation, can the con- ceptual factors be singled out.   None the less there is a quite definite limit to the extent to which the intuited can yield embodiment to categorial forms.   This is a matter to which I have already made reference.[1] Through intuitive sense-experience we can apprehend, in addition to the sensa, only shape, size, and motion. We can perceive neither substance nor causality, nor consequently, to take the more concrete forms in which these categories are scientifically specified, either mass or energy.   Mass and energy are ideal con- structions, necessary in order to account for what we experience, but never so appearing in their own persons that we can contemplate them face to face in the direct manner of shape, size, and motion.   Nor are they in the position of the interior parts of bodies, or even of the inner experiences which we impute to other selves. We can, on occasion, verify how the inner parts of bodies are arranged, and in our own persons, feelings and conations are directly experienced.   But mass and energy in the physical realm, as likewise mental powers and dispositions in the psychical realm, are in an altogether different position.   They can only be arrived at through the processes of ideal construction.   That is to say, they can only be thought, and can never be either sensed or intuited.   Our thinking of them,

[1] Cf. above, pp. 132-3.

though directed by the categorial forms which they serve to specify, is indeed based upon the data of experience; but however manifold be the data, and however reliable be the processes by which the ideal constructions are built up, they must to the end remain outside the provinces of intuition and of inner experience.   We are not merely imputing to this or that reality what we otherwise or elsewhere experience; we are discerning what to the end continues to be discernible only by this method.   But if so, must not such thinking be regarded as, so to speak, creative—*i.e.* as proceeding by a method of metaphysical *postulation*[1]—and if it be thus creative, can it at the same time legitimately be regarded as revealing, like sensing and intuiting, the nature of the independently real? Before attempting to answer this difficult question, we must determine more precisely the nature of those categories which conform to the type of substance and causality.

The very generally recognised fact that substance and causality stand in the closest possible connection with one another would seem to be due to the connection of both with the category of whole and part, which is, in fact, the basis of all other categories.   For just as the category of necessitation signifies the relation whereby a whole is a whole relatively to its parts, namely, as determining them, substance would appear to signify the correlative aspect whereby these parts go to constitute the whole which thus determines them. However a whole may condition its parts, it must be a whole *of* parts, and in the absence of the parts would

[1] *I.e.* making postulates for which experience affords no grounds—a method which Mr. Alexander and Mr. Whitehead are very rightly emphatic in rejecting.

not be a whole or indeed exist in any form.   To this
extent the relation is reciprocal; and in so far, though
not further or otherwise, the parts are *self*-subsistent.
Had this connection in which substance always stands
to the whole that acts as its environment been kept
more consistently in view, philosophy might have
avoided many of the deceptive short-cuts by which it
has sought to attain its goal.   Just as the part is
necessitated to be what it is through the whole which
it goes to constitute and uphold, so it can only be
understood in terms of what lies ' outwith '[1] itself.
However ' substantial ' and ' self-subsistent,' to the
end it remains a part, and by that we must mean that
it is ingredient throughout the range of its conditions and effects, and that however partial it may
itself be, these cannot fall short of the whole within
which they are found.[2]   The parts can have existence
only through participation in the wholeness of the
whole; they cannot be self-subsistent in any sense
which prevents their being in equal degree self-
transcendent.   This is quite evident when we are
dealing with whole and part in its strictly temporal
or spatial aspect.   Modern mathematics may define
a continuum as being composed of points, but it at
once adds that they constitute a ' compact ' series,
such that between any two points other points can
always be found to exist.   In other words, an analysis
of the continuum can never reduce it to a countable
number of self-subsistent points.   The points are
positions, and positions have meaning only by reference
to the series or other wholes within which they are

[1] I use this Scotticism as conveying a meaning more exact than the
term ' outside.'

[2] Cf. the passage quoted from Mr. Whitehead, above, p. 7 *n*.

discriminated. That this is no less true of substance in all its possible applications is what I here venture to suggest.[1]

Owing to the close connection in which substance and causality stand to one another, similar remarks are equally applicable to the latter. If necessitation refers to the manner in which a whole determines its constituent parts, the very usual view of causation as consisting in a relation between two substances or two events, or even between two distinct sets of conditions, will have to be reconsidered. If substances and events are, as we must recognise, in all cases embedded in, and constituted by, the wider wholes which make them what they are, no causal action can draw its resources exclusively from any such narrowly delimited existences. When causal agency or connection is viewed in the above manner the causal relation becomes unintelligible, and does violence to the continuities which are so fundamental a feature of all natural occurrences. Causal agency, like substance, always transcends the bounds of that in which it is immediately located; and to comprehend either we must reckon with the context and environment with which they are indissolubly bound up. I do not challenge Hume's main thesis, that the agency, as agency, transcends our means (at least present means) of knowledge. But if the more concrete standpoint be adopted, much in his method of stating his argument will call for alteration of a quite radical character.

---

[1] How ' open ' or how ' closed ' the Universe may be, I am not here intending to prejudge. Cf. above, pp. 141-3.

(e) The Limits within which Immediate Experience is enclosed

At this point we are called upon to consider, more fully than we have yet done, the limits within which immediate experience is enclosed, and the manner in which thought, in ideal construction, enables the mind to transcend these limits and so to apprehend reality in its wider and deeper aspects.

The range allowed to immediate experience, *on the objective side*, is determined by the extent to which Nature can manifest itself through the features of size, shape, motion, and the sensa. Whatever in Nature is not expressed *in* these features, though its fuller nature may for thought be expressed *through* them (as, *e.g.*, its solidity or ' materiality ' through sensations of resistance),[1] does not allow of being sensuously experienced. It can only be reached through ideal construction. Mass and energy are subject to this limitation.[2]

On the subjective side, these limits are determined by the extent to which the mind can immediately experience its own states and processes; and this, as it would seem, it can do only in feeling and conation, *i.e.* in processes of ' enjoyment.' Processes of cognition or awareness, *i.e.* all forms of consciousness which are not feelings or conations,[3] are processes which we

---

[1] ' Matter ' is a more or less popular term, denoting what, from the scientific point of view, are highly complex physical entities. Its presence is determined, for ordinary consciousness, primarily by sensations of contact and resistance.

[2] On this subject, cf. Stout's *Manual of Psychology*, 3rd ed. p. 18 ff.

[3] I am here retaining the usual distinction between the three aspects of conscious experience: (1) awareness as a term equivalent to the term cognition, (2) feeling, and (3) conation. Consciousness and awareness are not, therefore, synonymous terms.

postulate in view of certain changes in, and features of, the field of the sensuously experienced and of the thought-about—a field which, of course, includes the ' enjoyed ' feelings and conations. In other words, we have no awareness of awareness, any more than we directly contemplate mass or energy. Awareness is indeed as fundamental in the psychical life as physical science shows energy to be in the natural world. For to allege that we are never aware of awareness is not to assert that we know nothing about it; we know a great deal about it. Awareness can, for instance, be defined as an essentially *contemplative* process, and yet as not merely a passive capacity of being ' modified ' (whatever that may mean) by the objects to which it is ' directed ' (another term really meaningless in this connection).[1] It must, it would seem, be highly complex, involving the apprehension of those fundamental meanings that are necessary to the intuition of time and space.

That such analyses are much more precarious than those by which in physical science the existence of mass and energy are demonstrated, I am not concerned to question. But that the difference is, in all essentials, a difference only in degree—due in the psychical field to the greater paucity of the data and to the greater complexity of what is being analysed—the physicist, in face of the present disturbing controversies in regard to his main ultimate concepts, will probably not care to deny.

Together with the processes of awareness, the psychologist is constrained to postulate a variety of

[1] On Mr. Alexander's ultra-realist view, the ' direction ' of awareness does, of course, have a very definite meaning; but I am speaking from a different standpoint.

special powers and dispositions.   Just as the physical is wider than the material, so the psychical is wider than the conscious.   For not only is the immensely greater proportion of the mind's possible conscious experiences, *e.g.* its memories, *not* in consciousness at any one moment; the powers and dispositions which *constitute* the self, for instance the capacities, partly innate, largely acquired, which form the individual's more or less abiding intellectual and moral character, cannot *ever* appear ' within the conscious field ' *in themselves*.   They determine our intellectual processes and our conduct, and they find expression in the feelings and conations, but only, we may say, in a manner analogous to that in which mass and energy reveal themselves in and through size, shape, motion, and the sensa, *i.e.* not directly in their own persons, but very efficiently, for all practical purposes, in the effects which in the directly experienced entities they *do* determine.

There are certain types of existence which cannot be exclusively referred either to the class of immediate experiences or to the class to which energy and mental dispositions belong, though like the latter they are reached by processes of ideal construction.   Such are the constituents into which science breaks up the larger bodies which alone are apprehensible in sense-experience, *i.e.* molecules, atoms, and electrons.   If we directly experience the larger bodies, then *ipso facto* we are directly experiencing their constituents— not with any completeness, but still in at least certain of their features, *e.g.* as to the portions of space within which they lie, the general shapes to which by their groupings and vibratory motions they give rise, and the translatory motions which, in composing a mass, they share in common. Also, these constituents are viewed as themselves possessing shapes and motions, in some degree analogous to those of the bodies which they compose. On this assumption we can in imagination picture molecules, atoms, and electrons; we can even construct enlarged models of what we conceive to be their groupings and spatial inter-relations.

The status of the ether is a more difficult question. On Kelvin's view of atoms as vortices in ether, the ether will so far be in much the same position as the atoms themselves. We shall be experiencing it directly in so far as we experience bodies which are made up of portions of the ether in this or that state of tension. We shall not, of course, thereby experience the ether in such manner as to be able, by direct inspection, to read off its properties and characteristics. But neither can we do this in regard to gross matter, *i.e.* read off the constitution and characteristics of molecules and atoms. Both matter and ether we know directly in the immediate experience of their behaviour, and therefore much in the manner in which we gather a man's abilities and character, *i.e.* his abiding capacities and dispositions, from his directly observed actions. In other words, we may say that we know molecules, atoms, and ether directly in certain of their characteristics, and through ideal construction as regards their other properties. These latter properties, in turn, are of two types, those which are expressible in terms of size, shape, or motion, and which therefore allow of being pictured in imagination, and so of being represented by a mechanical or diagrammatic device, and those which are reducible to or involve mass and energy. These

remarks will still hold, though with certain modifications, even when ether is interpreted, not on the
analogy of ' matter,' but in the manner of Whitehead,
as " an ether of events." For so long as the concept
of ether is employed at all in physical science, presumably it belongs to the same class of hypothetically
constructed entities as molecules, atoms, and electrons.

(f) Further Consideration of the Categories of Substance and Causality

The category of substance stands for the demand
that we find the *self-subsistent* (in the duly qualified
sense above noted),[1] and causality for the demand that
we find the really effective *agencies* (likewise in the
above qualified sense). Both categories are forms
whereby unity is sought: the former seeks this unity
in the abidingly existent, the latter in the changes
which the existent undergoes. Further, both categories obtain application in our experience only in
connection with sensa, that is, only where, and in so
far as, the continuities of time and space are differentiated through qualitative differences. For in substance we seek that which unifies different sensa, and
is the ground of their being experienced together, and
of their existing in this or that specific mode under this
or that set of conditions; and in causality we seek the
conditions which determine a qualitatively characterised event to take the place of another event of different
character.

We may, in the light of results established by the
sciences, come to recognise that the qualities are sensa,
and so to regard them as events and not as attributes

----

[1] Pp. 163-5.

of bodies, but we do not thereby succeed in eliminating
all qualitative differences even from the mechanical
sphere. For when the secondary qualities are thus
transferred to another plane of occurrence, their place
is taken by the various forms of energy; and, as we
have noted, energy is a type of existence not picturable
in imagination, and never capable of exhaustive definition, though progressively defined, as regards certain
of its modes of behaviour, in the light of the data
supplied by direct experience.

This, it would seem, is one main ground of the
problematic character of the categories. For since
energy enters into all instances of substance and
causality that are localisable in the physical realm, and
is indeed (though not as opposed to, but as involving
mass) their most fundamental factor, it confers on the
unities which we seek to define by means of these
categories its own abidingly problematic character.
If we cannot profess to comprehend how any one
type of energy can exist abidingly in ' one ' place or
' one ' thing; if, that is to say, ' potential ' energy be
definable only through the effects which follow when
certain conditions are realised, we cannot hope to
comprehend how a number of different potential
energies—colour, heat, chemical energies, etc.—are
united in substance. And when the no less problematic factor, that of mass, is recognised, this conclusion is the more fully confirmed.

Similarly, as regards causality, in determining the
manner in which one form of energy passes into
another, we can directly observe only those characteristics which take the form of size, shape, motion, and
the sensa. The energy as energy, and therefore the
process as genuinely active or causal, eludes our appre-

hension.   We continue to *think* it, and endeavour through observation of its effects to *locate* it.   We likewise endeavour to obtain as complete a knowledge as possible of its varying modes of behaviour, not only in all the possible types of situation in which it can be found to exist, but also in all those in which by experimental interference it can be made to exist.   We may indeed say that in the end by these means this and that form of energy becomes as well known to us as does the self; and how high and valuable a type of comprehension that is, will be admitted by all.   But to state the situation in this way is simply to recognise that the kind of limitation imposed on our present knowledge of nature extends in similar fashion to our knowledge of mind.   The unity and ultimate nature of the self is certainly not less mysterious than that of objects; its active agency, when it calls up an image of a past event, or when it brings about bodily movement, in order to be ' understood,' would demand, in addition to the solution of specifically psychical problems, the solution of those very physical problems which we have just been considering, and that in the highly complex forms in which they present themselves in the physiological sciences.

But to return to our main point: when, on the scientific level sensa are no longer regarded, in naïve fashion, as properties of material bodies, but as themselves independent natural events, we have a further problem, that of ' causally ' correlating them with the various physical and physiological processes upon which they supervene.[1]   Herein, even more patently

---

[1] Cf. Whitehead, *The Concept of Nature*, pp. 97-8 : " In natural science ' to explain ' means merely to discover ' interconnexions.'   For example, in one sense there is no explanation of the red which we see.   It is red, and

than in our causal correlation of different types of energy, the establishment of continuity of process— an ideal after which the scientist is ever striving—has, at one stage or another, to give place to a simple correlation of non-continuous happenings.

This, however, it is important to note, is not a mere *failure* of explanation, a stopping short in the scientific analysis, owing to lack of data or to limitation of scientific technique.   Continuity, as we have to recognise, is but one of the two conflicting ideals of unity which inspire the scientist in his search for knowledge.   The other ideal is represented by the categories of substance and causality, expressive the one of the relative independence of the self-subsistent, and the other of the relative independence involved in being an active agent.   In proportion as *complete* continuity is established, these types of existence lose their specific characters, and reality is thereby proportionately impoverished.   The only existence then allowed is that typified by the *continuance* of a motion not interfered with; the only occurrence recognised is that of *transition* from the same to the same.   Substance, and also activity in the sense of any advance into novelty, are entirely eliminated.   When the establishment of

---

there is nothing else to be said about it.   Either it is posited before you in sense-awareness or you are ignorant of the entity red.   But science has explained red.   Namely it has discovered interconnexions between red as a factor in nature and other factors in nature, for example, waves of light which are waves of electro-magnetic disturbances.   There are also various pathological states of the body which lead to the seeing of red without the occurrence of light waves.   Thus connexions have been discovered between red as posited in sense-awareness and various other factors in nature.   The discovery of these connexions constitutes the scientific explanation of our vision of colour."   Cf. Broad on the relative character of the distinction between causation and creation, *Scientific Thought*, pp. 535-44, partially quoted above, pp. 92-3.

such continuity is conceived as an ideal in scientific explanation, the differentiating factors are all the time being taken for granted. It is tacitly, but inconsistently, assumed that the differentiations will still in some manner persist when the goal is attained. Indeed we can observe, in the history of the sciences, a certain tendency to alternate between the two ideals. At one time discreteness, as in the chemical analysis of seemingly continuous bodies, is mainly emphasised and progressively established; and even the ether may then be viewed as a gas.[1] On the other hand, when this method of explanation has been carried to a certain point, the opposite tendency reasserts itself, and the discrete existences, atoms or electrons, are viewed as being but differentiations of an etheric medium regarded as continuous. These opposite tendencies illustrate the twofold requirements which, as I have already emphasised, are prescribed by any ideal of unity that is genuinely to fulfil the demands voiced through the fundamental category of totality. There can be no totality if there be no parts; and there can be no parts if the self-subsistent be disallowed. In other words, there must be differentiations of content if there is to be a wholeness which is more than merely that which belongs to each and every portion of a continuous series or medium. On the other hand, there can be no parts, and therefore nothing self-subsistent, save in and through a whole which supplies the wider context and the conditioning environment necessary thereto. Accordingly any complete reduction to continuity, if genuine and not merely apparent, signifies only that in some particular case factors, which appear in correla-

[1] As by Mendeléeff.

tion with, or as bearers of, the continuous process, can
for the purposes in hand be left out of account.   This
is what happens when the process whereby energy is
communicated from one body to another is treated as
a continuous process.   The two bodies, as bearers
of the motion and as sequent ' owners ' of the energy,
are ignored.   There is no *causal* activity, not only
because there is nothing to act, but also because there
is really no change such as demands causal agency for
its occurring.   The energy, viewed as a process of
actual motion, has, so to speak, been personified, as
being an entity in and by itself, and therefore as continuing to be what presumably it has unchangingly
all along been, namely, a vibratory or translatory
motion.   Such a method of procedure may be justified
by its fruits when the scientist has in mind, say,
the principle of the conservation of energy, *i.e.* of
its equivalence with itself *in quantity* throughout
all its possible transformations.   In such an inquiry
the precise nature and conditions of the transformations are not relevant considerations, and can therefore be left out of account.   But as the principle, in
its employment of the term ' transformation,' itself
indicates, the other features, though abstracted from,
are not denied, still less disproved.   In other inquiries,
as in chemical analysis, their consequences and effects
are among the direct subjects of study.

To return now to the question, above raised,[1] as to
whether in employing the concepts of substance and
active agency we are not indulging in a type of metaphysical postulation for which experience can afford
no evidence.   My answer, as already suggested,[2] is
that so far are these concepts from being at a certain

---

[1] P. 163.   [2] P. 134 ff.

stage in knowledge—whether at the animistic stage or later through the Greek philosophers [1]—introduced as ungrounded postulates, to obviate difficulties which ought never to have been raised, that on the contrary only in and through them can ordinary sense-experience be acquired. Metaphysical postulation—if the processes by which we thus round out our experience may be so described—is legitimate, because only as metaphysically oriented is the human type of consciousness possible at all; [2] only by transcending the immediate can it apprehend the immediate. The function of the fundamental categories (whole and part, necessitation) is to endow the mind with the capacity to apprehend certain universal meanings which are indispensable for the intuition of time and space. These categories are apprehended in and through our awareness of the latter; and though they must be further specified before they take the forms of substance and causality, this specification is only such as they themselves prescribe, in their relation to the other aspects of sense-experience.

What goes far to justify the attack upon ‘metaphysical postulation’ is the assumption which has generally gone along with it, that not only can substance and causality be *located* in this and that portion of space, in this and that set of events, but

[1] Mr. Whitehead would seem to ascribe their introduction mainly to Aristotle. Cf. *The Concept of Nature*, pp. 16-18, 24.

[2] Cf. Stout, *Some Fundamental Points in the Theory of Knowledge* (St. Andrews University Quincentenary Publications, 1911), p. 21 : “ Thought, as such, has for its ultimate object the universe in its unity; but not, of course, the universe in all its detail. The special features emerge successively, leaving a relatively indefinite background. The unity of the universe is apprehended in apprehending its parts as being partial—as being incomplete and requiring completion through their relations within a whole which transcends them.”

that the categories, in and by themselves, yield a more than purely formal insight into their nature. Such positive insight, as I have argued, is only possible in proportion as empirical data—thus far all too limited in extent and type—are available for the purpose.

CHAPTER VIII

SENSE AND INTUITION

We may now proceed to a question, the consideration of which I have hitherto been deferring, and upon which much remains to be said; how, if visual and other sensa be not in themselves extended, we yet apprehend them as spread-out; or to state the question in reverse fashion: how the intuited comes to be apprehended in terms of the sensed. If the sensa and extension be really, in their intrinsic nature, independent of one another, how come they to be thus, in our experience, inseparably interconnected? It must also be explained how intuition can be distinct from sensing, and yet at the same time be a direct, face-to-face apprehension of the independently real.

(i.) Preliminary Considerations

The reasons which I have given for adopting the above positions are, in the main, threefold. In the first place, the sensa are, it would seem, complexly conditioned by antecedent physical and physiological processes, and as thus occurring as terminal members in very lengthy series cannot be known to be qualities inherent in the physical objects in which the series originate. Just as sound cannot be known to be *in*

178

a bell, so the redness of a red book cannot be asserted
to be spread out over the covers of the book. The
position usually adopted by subjectivist thinkers is
that the redness, though not in the book, may none
the less have a spreadoutness proper to itself. This
view I am unable to accept for the further, second,
reason, that if extensity be thus allowed to visual
sensa, the space which we contemplate will not be real
space, but a duplicate, and that in consequence all
the difficulties of a thoroughly subjectivist position
will be on our hands. Then thirdly, and lastly, this
position has likewise to be rejected for the reason
that space being what it is, it cannot be apprehended,
in the manner of colour, by a process of sensing.
It is, it would seem, an object not of sense but of an
intuition in which categorial thinking plays an indispensable part. That wherein it does agree with
colour is, we may believe, that the process of its apprehension, however complexly conditioned, is genuinely
contemplative, yielding knowledge of the independently
real. Just as we contemplate a sensum face to face,
and know it for what it is—a constituent in a public
world, though, for assignable reasons, directly known
only by one percipient—so we intuite space in its
actual, unique nature, as a fundamental feature of
the real.

As I have also already pointed out,[1] on this view
the brain has two very different functions: on the one
hand, as conditioning the sensa; and on the other
hand, as conditioning the various processes, sensing,
intuiting, and categorial thinking, whereby the sensa
and all other factors are apprehended.

These, then, being the reasons which constrain us

[1] Above, pp. 79-80.

to hold that the colour-sensa, in agreement with all other sensa, are extensionless, I may now proceed to indicate the manner in which I should propose to meet the many and obvious difficulties to which this position gives rise.

My problem may be stated to be that of showing how sensing and intuiting, notwithstanding their diversity of nature, co-operate in making possible the contemplative process whereby coloured space reveals itself to the mind.[1] That we experience colour only as extended and visual space only as coloured is the agreed datum, of which the subjectivist and the intuitive theories are competing explanations. On the subjectivist view, the space so apprehended is a private space, distinct from that of the natural world. On the view which I am defending, real, independent space, in its own person, is here making entry into the ' conscious field.' Both views run counter to the beliefs of ordinary consciousness. On the subjectivist view, we suffer from an illusion when we believe, as the unsophisticated always do, that the space which the colour occupies is portion of an independent space. But on that type of intuitive view which I am endeavouring to formulate we are committed to a seemingly much more paradoxical consequence, namely, that we are almost certainly subject to an illusion when we believe, as again the unsophisticated always do, that colour really occupies the space *in which it is seen*. The reality which is thus seen must, indeed, have some positive properties of its own; and just possibly it may be coloured, and

---

[1] Since the objections to the position which I am defending are at their strongest in regard to colour, any answer which I can give will apply, *a fortiori*, to other types of sensa.

may even have the particular colour which it is seen
as having; in all probability, however, it has not.
I may be able, in some degree, to tone down this
unqualified statement, that a sensum is never where
it is seen—if sensa be not in space, are they not as
correctly seen in one space as in any other?—but in
substance it must stand.

(a) *The Associationist Hypothesis*

I may now make my thesis more definite. The
view commonly held in associationist psychology, from
the time of Locke [1] onwards, is that the mind at each
moment constructs out of the given sensa, with the aid
of revived sensa connected therewith, the time and
space world of ' immediate ' experience. A well-nigh
incredible elaborateness of construction is thus postulated as being carried out by the mind, and as having
to be achieved anew at each moment. Now if the views
for which I have been contending can be accepted, no
such excessive burden need be imposed upon the
mind. For if our awareness of what is public cannot
be accounted for as due solely to awareness of sensa,
but demands the co-operation of factors not contained
in, or revealed by, the sensa, a much simpler machinery
will suffice. If there is consciousness of time and
space whenever there is consciousness at all, may we
not reasonably expect that the constant factors will
have conditions, physiological and psychical, distinct
from, and supplementary to, those which condition
apprehension of the ever-changing sensa? Why should
the constant be regarded as ever-renewed, and not
rather as economically provided for in some constant

1 Cf. below, p. 183, note 2.

way. When a letter of more or less uniform import
has to be addressed to a large number of people with
differing requirements, we find it convenient to have
a fixed form printed, with blanks for the names and
other varying items. This is preferable to the re-
composing and rewriting of each separate epistle.
Surely Nature may be expected to have hit upon so
obvious an economy as this, and not to have laid
upon the brain and mind the enormous and useless
strain of creating ever anew out of the varying sensa
of the moment the fixed and constant features that are
always there when anything at all is being apprehended.
Does not the associationist hypothesis appear un-
natural, the more we think of it?   On the lower levels
of vegetable and animal life, Nature's devices are,
indeed, not infrequently extravagantly wasteful; but
as she advances to the higher reaches, her methods,
just in proportion as they become the more effective,
are characterised, in equal degree, by the more
economical adaptation of means to ends.

When, further, we observe that consciousness
always involves the thought of more than is perceived, and that only by reference to a wider reality
than is being sensuously apprehended is consciousness possible at all, the associationist theory displays
another and yet more serious defect. That the sensa
of our developed consciousness demand for their
apprehension a setting or context supplementary to
themselves, the associationists are, of course, very well
aware. This supplement, additional to the sensa,
but demanded in apprehension of the sensa, they
regard as consisting in the revival of past experiences. But such a position implies that consciousness begins as being awareness of single sensa, and

only becomes complex in proportion as experience
develops.   As already argued,[1] analysis of our consciousness of time suffices to disprove this view.   If
the ' now ' cannot be apprehended save in a context
of the ' no longer ' and the ' not yet,' revival of past
experiences will not account for such a mode of awareness.   This type of context is a type which must in
its main features be present in every case; and it is
therefore as little capable of being accounted for in
terms of past as in terms of present sensa.

The plausibility of the associationist theory is partly
due to our readiness to accept the fundamental assumption upon which Locke proceeds in his *Essay*, namely,
that by the method of *analysis* we can discover the
elements out of which the existing complexes have
arisen.   This assumption finds fruitful application in
physics and chemistry, but it should not without due
precautions be carried over into the biological and
psychological fields.   The simple, or apparently simple,
sensations into which we can decompose our complex
perceptions are, Locke declares, the units out of which
all experience has been built up, and through the
aggregation of which it has developed.[2]   Might we
not as well argue that the cross-section of a mature
chicken reveals to us, in the various bones and tissues,
the diverse original components out of which it has
been pieced together?   To take such a view is to adopt
one-half of the mediaeval view of growth, according to
which the various parts of an oak, roots, trunk, and
branches, exist in the acorn, without the other half

---

[1] Cf. above, pp. 82-3.

[2] Though Locke cannot correctly be regarded as the father of associa-
tionism, he has exercised considerable influence upon its development, and
not least on this particular point.

which alone makes it consistent, namely, that a minia-ture oak exists complete in the acorn, that the seed is already at the start just as complex as that into which it passes, and that growth is therefore only increase in size. When we reject such mediaeval fancies and conform our views to the evidence, as now known, we have to recognise that the parts of a mature organism are as much products of growth and development as is the organism itself, and that nothing really similar to them need be found in the seed or germ-plasm from which they have been differentiated.

Owing to the fact that the egg of a chicken can be studied as well as the chicken itself, this fundamental fact has all along been appreciated in biology; but since the mind of the new-born child can be studied only very indirectly through its behaviour, the ab-surdities of the associationist psychology have per-sisted even to our own day. Even Herbert Spencer, though he appreciated the bearings of the biological standpoint, was so unduly influenced by the atomistic hypotheses prevailing in the physical sciences, that he attempted a grotesque blending of the two views, regarding our conscious experiences as simply so many permutations and combinations of an elementary and *unchanging* mental unit—a unit too simple to be any longer experienced separately by us, but which he conjecturally described as being of the nature of a simple ' shock ' sensation.

Atoms are no longer regarded by the physicist and chemist as being simple in constitution; nor are they any longer spoken of, in the manner of Tyndall and Huxley, as being " the foundation-stones " of the material Universe. The analytic method continues

to bear good fruit in these fields, but it need no longer
be viewed as the type of explanation to which every
science, even that of psychology, ought to conform.

(b) The Structure and Complex Constitution
of the Psychoplasm

The main difficulties of the view which I am
endeavouring to propound begin when we inquire
how awareness of time, space, and the categories can
be possible, if it be not acquired through the sensa;
and in meeting these difficulties I shall again make use
of a doctrine propounded by Mr. Ward—the doctrine
of ' psychoplasm,' as expounded in his *Psychological
Principles*.[1]

" As bioplasm, not a concourse of atoms, is for the present
the limiting term for biology, so we may speak of psychoplasm,
and not a ' manifold of sensations ' or ' mindstuff ' as our present
limit in psychology. Of the more ultimate nature of either
plasm, of the precise relations of the one to the other, or of the
relation of life in the physiological sense to experience or life
in the psychological sense, on all these points, we certainly
know little and need for the present say nothing. But
the analogy between biogenesis and psychogenesis is both
indisputable and striking: we have several times been led
incidentally to note it. Genesis in both cases implies a unity
that is shaped from within—a conception, be it observed, that
is essentially non-mechanical."

Mr. Ward, owing to the influence of his somewhat
monadistic view of the soul or knowing subject, takes
the term psychoplasm as referring only to the objective
content of experience, *i.e.* to the presentational continuum.[2] I shall take it as applying to the subjective
factors, the powers, dispositions, and processes by

---

[1] P. 412.   Cf. pp. 417, 424-6, 429.   [2] Cf. *op. cit.* p. 424.

means of which this continuum is apprehended; and so as representing an alternative to the associationist standpoint.

" [The] crude [associationist] psychology, obsolescent in this country since the article ' Psychology ' of the ninth edition of the *Encyclopædia Britannica*, may fairly be regarded now as obsolete.   Mental processes are not grouped into wholes by association but are distinguishable processes within a mental continuum.   The agglutinative conception of mind is replaced by the organic one.   Mind has its structure and constitution as an animal body has." [1]

As Mr. Ward proceeds to point out,[2] since the bioplasm is continuous throughout the successive generations, and so in the offspring is continuous with that of the parents, we may conjecture that on the side of the psychoplasm, as on the side of the bioplasm, the individual comes heir to a complex and rich inheritance.   The subjective continuum, in and through which consciousness originates, and the objective continuum which is thereby apprehended, may well, from the start, have a complexity in some degree corresponding to the bioplasm that organically conditions the possibility of the former.

The general character of this complexity has already been indicated.   Since consciousness is incapable of existing save in so far as there is a field of which it is aware, and since time, space, and certain categorial relations are elements invariably present in this field, we are justified in arguing that consciousness, on its subjective side, must be correspondingly complex. To apprehend the immediate, it must be able to transcend the immediate; in order to intuite the

---

[1] Alexander, *Space, Time and Deity*, vol. ii. p. 13.
[2] *Op. cit.* p. 424 ff.

specific characters of time and space, it must be equipped for apprehending certain universal meanings, and as involved in these latter the fundamental categories.

When we examine these uniform elements, time, space, and the categories, we find that they agree in one main feature, namely, in being formal. They are not contents, but only forms for the organisation of contents highly variable in their characters. This is why, for the possibility of experience, a further factor, that obtained through the process of sensing, is equally indispensable. There can be no awareness save on the occasion, as well as in terms, of sensa.

Our conscious experience is thus a function of two distinct factors, each of which must have its own specific set of conditions, and in accordance therewith its own appropriate value. Through the constant factors a public world is revealed; through the sensa, in terms of which alone this public world can be actually experienced, it is apprehended in a perspective suited to the individual's practical needs.

This distinction connects with the twofold function of the brain to which I have already referred; its function as conditioning awareness, and its function as conditioning the occurrence of sensa. In the former aspect the brain appears to function in a constant and uniform manner, corresponding to the uniform public character of the world which by so functioning it enables us to apprehend. In its other aspect the brain conditions the ever-changing, discontinuous, qualitatively varying sensa, which are private to the individual, and which, as such, are appropriate for enabling him to apprehend the public world in a perspective as unique as are his instinctive and other needs. Each of the two factors has its own rôle to play, and in the absence of either awareness would not occur.

Another way of stating this position is the following. What we apprehend is, in all cases, a complex situation. Within this complex situation we discriminate the contents of what it is usual to call our sensations. But as these contents are discriminated *within* the situation, they cannot be the materials out of which the situation *as a whole* is constructed. A whole cannot be constructed out of a selection of its own constituent parts. Indeed, the sense-contents can, it would seem, come into existence at all only under the conditions which the situation itself supplies. If there be no vibrating body and no air, no ear with its inner labyrinthine structure and no brain connected therewith, there will be no sounds. If the light of the sun, consisting in wave vibrations, does not act on the retina and through it on the occipital lobes, no colours will emerge. The sensa are events determined by, and happening within, the space-time situation; and to make them possible, the total situation is required. All that we are therefore justified in saying is that we come to apprehend the situation in terms of certain of the events which occur within it.

If we seek some other body of sense-material out of which the situation *as a whole* may be constructed, then with Kant we must postulate a manifold more comprehensive than, and different from, the data of the special senses. But this surely is a needless and perverse procedure! Kant, it would seem, himself only does so owing to the subjectivist manner in which his phenomenalism, very different though it may be from the subjectivism of Berkeley and his like, is still propounded.   If we adopt an out-and-out realist position, no such postulate need be made.   Independent reality will then be regarded as directly apprehended, that is, as making entry, not by proxy but in its own person, into the ' field of consciousness.'

In this way we avoid Descartes' subjectivist mode of interpreting the difference between the primary and the secondary qualities of bodies, as being an opposition between qualities that are independently real and qualities that are states of the mind.   Instead we bifurcate reality so as to set only awareness on the one side, and all contents, including the sensa, on the other. The private character of the sensa is then explicable without assumption of their subjectivity.

That consciousness, notwithstanding its complex character, should function so uniformly, and should, like white sunlight, conceal under a seeming simplicity the complexity of the processes in which it consists, is, as already suggested,[1] entirely in keeping with Nature's ordinary procedure.   All Nature's simplicities, whether of constitution or of function, mask the well-nigh incredible complexity of the manifold contributory factors which make them possible.   Consciousness, like instinct, yields to introspection no insight into the conditions which make it actual; but this is no ground for regarding either of them as supplying the conditions of its own existence.   The uniform character of consciousness, so far from justifying any inference as to simplicity in its conditions, points the other way. The ease and simplicity of motion in a centipede, the act of sneezing in a new-born child (involving, as the physiologist assures us, the acrobatic feat of co-ordinating some sixty or more muscles), are the

[1] Above, pp. 14, 33 ff.

outcome of inherited mechanisms in the nervous system of the insect and of the child, and accordingly are more complexly conditioned than any other known types of natural occurrence. The conditions of our sense-experience are not, I believe, exclusively physiological; but they are at least, we may safely conclude, highly manifold and complex.

Again, that the brain should have two such very different functions as that of conditioning awareness and that of conditioning the sensa, is also in line with Nature's general mode of behaviour. It delights, often quite grotesquely, in employing one and the same organ for both lower and higher purposes. The tongue, for instance, while serving as an organ for speech, is likewise the organ of taste, and as an instrument indispensable in the act of swallowing and in cleansing the mouth, has functions still humbler in character. The functions of the brain are, indeed, so far as we can discover, always exercised simultaneously. This, however, does not cause any practical inconvenience. On the contrary, such simultaneous exercise of the two functions is the very condition of effective control of environment, constraining us, as it does, in being conscious of the public world, to apprehend it in a perspective uniquely suited to our spatial standpoint and personal needs. Though this does, of course, throw obstacles in the way of our acquiring exact knowledge of the independent nature of the material world, none the less, even here, as I have already pointed out, Nature attains two diverse ends through a single set of instruments. Sense-perception, in man as in the animals, though primarily a strictly practical device for the purposes of adaptation, subserves, no less effectively, the very different function of making possible the progressive acquisition of scientific insight.

As already noted,[1] the primary function of the sensa is to define a personal perspective, suited to the percipient's personal standpoint and individual needs. They determine the extent to which, the limits under which, and the specific modes in which the primary qualities are sensuously apprehended. As experience shows, where there are no secondary qualities, there is never sense-experience in any form. Through gustatory, olfactory, and auditory sensa we apprehend objects as conditioning taste, odour, and sound; through cutaneous and motor sensa as having temperature and as being solid or material (*i.e.* as resistant), through visual sensa as connected with light and colour. Owing to the fact that the individual acquires his experience by the instrumentality of an animal organism, it is only thus in terms of secondary qualities, and under the limitations determined by them, and in the modes which they admit, that independent objects are initially apprehended.

(c) Anticipation in Pictorial Terms of Later Argument

If I may be allowed to anticipate my later argument by suggesting, in a crude, pictorial manner, the kind of answer which I shall ultimately give to the question before us, what occurs when we have sense-experience of objects may be described somewhat as follows. Consciousness, in virtue of the complex dispositions which constitute the mind's capacity of apprehension, has as the field of its observation independent reality in time and space. But this conscious-

---

[1] Cf. above, p. 32 ff.

ness comes into action only when aroused by sensa, private to each individual. It then, as it were, paints this or that portion of uniform time-space in the pigments which these sensa supply. Thus when I seem to myself to see a reflected object as behind a mirror, what I do is to paint the space which I intuite as behind the mirror with the colour-sensa which I am experiencing at the moment, and so to make the space behind the mirror sensible to the mind. It *is* the space behind the mirror which is then seen; we are indeed seeing it erroneously, as we find when we bring the same sense to bear under altered conditions, or under the same conditions test the first experience by another sense, such as touch. But the use here made of the sensa does not differ in general character from that to which we put them when we see a book as red or the matter in bodies as being continuous. In all three cases the interpretation is determined by considerations of convenience, and can be corrected in terms of experience which the sensa themselves enable us to acquire. In the first case the error can be, and is corrected, in the light of ordinary experience; in the other two cases in the light of experience sought out experimentally by the scientist.

From this standpoint, as we have likewise already noted,[1] a reason can be given why we should be able to apprehend objects only in terms of sensa which are *not* their inherent qualities, namely, that our senses function in subordination to the needs of a type of experience which is telepathic in character. Through the senses, as continued into the brain, we come to apprehend what is happening either at a distance from the body, or in the case of organic sensa at a

---

[1] Cf. above, p. 34.

distance from the brain, and (what is of fundamental importance for self-preservation alike among the animals and in man) in a *personal* perspective that exactly corresponds to the unique relations in which the observer stands to objects far and near. For this latter purpose sensa, *private* to each individual, and so the better varying with his unique personal viewpoint, are a very suitable arrangement. Colour enables us to determine direction, to distinguish at a glance the outline of an object as it stands out against its differently coloured background — we can conceive no means by which this would be possible in the absence of colour—to discriminate distance according to brightness or dimness of colouring, and so forth. In terms of colour-differences we are thus enabled telepathically to apprehend distance, shape, and size. Sound warns us of movements, and unlike colour enables us to apprehend what is behind our backs, as well as of what is in front, and by its variations to reveal both direction and distance. It also admirably supplements sight owing to its serviceability in the dark as well as in the light. Similar advantages justify the existence and employment of the other types of sensa. In this, as in other ways, the biological sciences afford a large body of circumstantial evidence in support of the view here taken of the ontological status and empirical function of the sensa.

But what need, it will be said, to regard the senses as functioning in this telepathic manner, if, as I have insisted, it is the very nature of consciousness to be self-transcendent, and to have as its field, not subjective or mental states, but an independent world in time and space. The answer may be given: first, that since

o

the mind can, out of its own resources, bring into operation only formal or categorial factors, it cannot experience time save in a concrete durational span, or intuite space save as sensibly embodied, and is therefore dependent throughout upon given sensa. We may be able—once we have acquired definite experience—to think, in formal, categorial terms, what cannot be sensed, but for first apprehension sensa are indispensable.

Further, if sense-experience is to be of any use to animals or to man, in their ordinary activities, it must be, not a contemplative apprehension of things as they are *in themselves*, not even if they be selectively simplified by being apprehended only in certain of their features and in part of their constitution, but an apprehension of them *in their relations to the self*. Only so can the necessary rapidity and adaptiveness of response be effectively attained. Other arrangements by which this could have been secured may be abstractly conceivable; but that the method actually followed is by way of special sensa, strictly private and physiologically (and possibly also in part psychically) generated, appears to be the most reasonable interpretation of the known facts.

(d) The Nature of ' Mental Images '

On this theory, by adoption of the view worked out by Mr. Alexander,[1] we can obtain a very simple solution of the important question as to how we apprehend those times which are too long past to fall within the specious present, and those spaces which

---

[1] *Space, Time and Deity*, vol. i. p. 97 ff., 113 ff. ; vol. ii. p. 83 ff., 218-19, 228-9.

are too distant to be cognised in terms of present
sensa.   No established psychological results stand in
the way of our assuming that images are identical in
character with sense-perceptions.   We may therefore
assume that in them, as in perception, sensa private
to the individual and physiologically conditioned constitute an essential factor.   Presumably these sensa
differ from those supplied in perception chiefly in
being proximately initiated not by stimuli acting on
the sense-organs, but by processes coming from other
parts of the brain.   Very probably they also differ as
regards intensity, steadiness, and duration, though, as
dreams, hallucinations, and the like appear to show,
even in these respects the differences are mainly due
to their incapacity to acquire, in ordinary waking
experience, a sensory background harmonious with
themselves.   Otherwise they seem to play a part exactly
analogous to that of the primary sensa.[1]   They are
employed by the mind to define and articulate public
time and public space.   When we picture previously
experienced happenings and existences, we paint the
past time and the distant space in terms of sensa
now being experienced by us.   These sensa are still
employed to render sensible and to particularise a
time and a space which they do not themselves reveal.
What we apprehend in and through them are not
mental or private objects, but the actual events of the
past which have been experienced by us in the past,
or which have been reported by others, and the
actual persisting objects which have been observed
by ourselves or others, and which, as we may in many

---

[1] If I am correct in regarding sensa as not 'qualities' but events, the
sensa of first experience and the so-called revived sensa must alike be
regarded as *one-time* occurrences.

cases have reason to know, still exist, in some distant space, continuous with the space of present sense-perception.   Just as when we see a now present but spatially distant object, we are experiencing the actual, real, independent object, so when I in Edinburgh picture St. Paul's Cathedral (previously seen) in London, what I am apprehending is the actual St. Paul's, and not any merely mental duplicate of it.   Similarly, when we picture to ourselves the past, we are picturing the actual past at the distance in time at which it actually occurred.   Of course in all cases there are the same unavoidable elements of sensory perspective, just as happens when I apprehend a drop of water through present vision, or discriminate the just past within the wider period of the specious present.[1]   In imagi-nation, as in sense-experience, consciousness of the public world and awareness of the sensa co-operate, each conditioning the possibility of the other.

(e) Intuition a Mode of Direct Contemplation

But I have not yet directly faced the fundamental difficulty which has been dogging our steps from the start, as to how sensing and intuiting, notwithstanding their very different characters and functions, are yet able to co-operate, or the still more serious difficulty how intuiting, thus regarded as distinct from sensing, can be capable of yielding direct knowledge of the independently real.

There is a preliminary difficulty which may be in the mind of the reader.   If only the sensa be directly sensed, and if, as has been argued, they yield, in and

---

[1] We have also to bear in mind how large a part revived sensa play even in what seems to be a purely sensory apprehension of what is here and now.

by themselves, no apprehension of time or of space,
are we not committed to the very unsatisfactory view
that everything over and above the sensa is merely
thought, and not experienced?   Thinking may be a
reliable means of knowledge; but what has to be
accounted for is not merely *knowledge* of time and
space, but that which we undoubtedly also possess,
actual *sense*-experience of them.

This objection is, however, based upon a misunderstanding; and I have mentioned it only in
order to emphasise my entire agreement with the
point of view from which it is propounded. I am
not attempting to argue that in experiencing the
sensa we mentally interpret them in terms of forms
which the mind supplies in the act of apprehension.
On the contrary, I am maintaining that it is public
time and public space which we directly intuite; and
that if we are to speak of 'mental interpretation,'
this phrase can only be applicable to the processes
whereby each percipient interprets these independent
existences in terms of his private sensa. For, as I
have been endeavouring to show, save in and through
the contemplation of time and space no consciousness
is possible. To reduce consciousness to the apprehension merely of sensa is, in effect, to abolish consciousness, and therefore to render incomprehensible
how we should ever acquire consciousness even of
the sensa. That is to say, on the view which I am
advocating, our apprehension of sensa as occurring
in time or as extended in space is not an addition
to the knowledge which the sensa yield. We do
not advance, by way of inference or interpretation,
from consciousness of sensa to consciousness of time
and space. The latter type of consciousness is a

condition of the former; and this being so, our apprehension of time and space must be as immediate and as strictly contemplative as is our awareness of the sensa themselves.   If time and space cannot be immediately apprehended, neither can the sensa.

Again, I am not simply asserting, in the manner of Kant, that time and space condition our *consciousness* of the sensa; I also desire to maintain, with equal insistence, that they condition the very occurrence of the sensa.   Only in a time-space world which allows of the required antecedent happenings, physical and physiological, can the complexly conditioned sensa obtain foothold in existence.   For if we admit that sensa, though always private to each percipient, are not for this reason subjective, but are objective happenings, there need be no difficulty in also admitting that they are events integral to the system of physical nature.   And this, obviously, is a very radical departure from the standpoint of subjectivism.   If the sensa be thus integral to the physical system, and are known directly, then to that extent we have an immediate apprehension of independent reality.   And since it can be shown that not only do sensa allow of this ' interpretation ' as occurring within a space-time world, but that in adopting it the human mind has successfully built up a coherent body of detailed knowledge in regard to the conditions of their occurrence and of their modes of existence, the realist interpretation of time and space may be regarded as holding the field.   Unless in approaching these problems we are to insist upon retaining those dualistic assumptions which have been usual since the time of Descartes, and which Kant, after all his efforts to overcome them, still left standing, we may well expect that since conscious

beings are integral to the real world, factors so fundamental as time and space will be found to play a
central rôle in all occurrences, whether of conscious
experience or of external nature. The *onus probandi*
must lie with those who venture to propound the
counter-thesis.

I have stated my reasons for refusing to recognise
spatiality as inherent in the visual or other sensa. One
other reason may here be mentioned—it prepares the
way for our further discussion — namely, that the
usual method of explanation will not apply in the
analogous case of time. Only the apprehension of
the *order* of the occurrence of sensa, not the apprehension of the *content* of this or that sensum, will yield
awareness of time. Time *envelops* the sensa, so to
speak, and in transcending each sensum, transcends
all the sensa; just as does space, on the view which
I am advocating. Time does, indeed, appear to be
more inextricably bound up with the sensa than is
space; admittedly they have duration, whereas we are
questioning whether any of them have extension.
But this difference can easily be exaggerated. If
sensa have to be regarded as actually occurring and
enduring in a time-order, they have likewise to be
regarded (or at least in physical science are so regarded)
as occurring in dependence upon events that are
spatially ordered. It will not, as already stated,
suffice to regard space and time as *interpretations* given
to the sensa. They must be more than that; they
must be intuited, *i.e.* contemplated. They must be
apprehended in a face to face manner, as actual components of independent reality.

(f) The Evolution of Sense-experience:
the Possible Alternative Views

But Nature begins the task of creating or liberating [1] consciousness on a very humble scale, and only advances to the human type after long preliminary preparation by the elaboration of animal forms. At all stages in this evolution, only that amount of consciousness is allowed which is necessary for the practical purposes of adaptation; and it is further tied down— time and space apart—to those particular features in the environment which are capable of acting on the organism, either, in the earliest stages, through its general sensitiveness, or, in the higher stages, through action upon the special organs of sense.

We are mainly concerned with the sense of sight. How it functions in the lower vertebrates when there is no yellow spot and no binocular vision, we can only conjecture. We cannot, with any precision, say how far, in these lower stages, colours are distinguished, or how far they are used in the discernment of outline, etc. But if Dr. Elliot Smith's very interesting theory [2] as to the origin of human intelligence, that it has come about in connection with, and as a result of, the development of binocular vision, be accepted, it will go some way towards explaining why our fundamental categories are so closely bound up with space, and why they can most easily be established and defined in this reference. It will also aid us in explaining how colour has come to be the mind's chief ally in the apprehension of size, shape, distance, and the like. In the

---

[1] I do not wish to raise the questions here involved.

[2] Cf. Presidential Address to the Anthropological Section of the British Association, Dundee, 1912.

earliest stages the function of visual sensa was not, probably, of this character. They doubtless served merely to discriminate between light and darkness, and in detecting the direction in which the light is located. Discrimination of colours may also, even apart from apprehension of definite spatial forms, have been of value in enabling an animal to recognise what is serviceable as food, and to react defensively against danger. But for appreciation through sight of spatial relations we must presuppose the mental capacity to apprehend outline as outline, *i.e.* to apprehend space in its essential complexity.

The capacity for spatial discrimination must already, however, prior to any high development of sight, have been present in connection with the sense of touch. It must at least have been present in the form of a capacity to locate contacts in the parts of the body from which they come. When we leave aside sight, we do indeed find it difficult to picture to ourselves how the mind can have apprehended the body, in its main parts and as a whole, in purely tactual terms. But this is merely a consequence of the predominance which sight has acquired in our imaginative activities; the capacities of the blind conclusively demonstrate that tactual sensa afford all the sense-data required for adequate apprehension of space-relations, and through combination of separate experiences for constructing images of the larger areas. In the cutaneous sensa there is, however, no such quite obvious fusion with spreadoutness as we find in the case of the visual sensa. Pressure, heat and cold have an ambiguous character — agreeing therein with tastes and odours, and even with sounds — which renders it difficult to decide how far their connection with space really extends. We may observe

that it was not until the associationists had failed in
their attempts to account for our apprehension of
space from extensionless sensa, and until Kant had
also failed to explain it by means of forms contributed
by the mind, that the psychologists bethought themselves of asserting the possibility that extensity may
be a property belonging to each single sensum.   This
in itself affords good evidence that the extensity, at
least of certain types of sensa, is by no means beyond
question.   In developed experience all sensa, owing to
the intuitive character of the complex perceptions into
which they have been taken up, have indeed acquired
a more or less direct connection with space.   That
such extensity as they may have, or appear to have, can
be due exclusively to this source, always, therefore,
remains as an open possibility.   In any case the issue
cannot be decided simply by direct inspection of the
sensa, as they now present themselves.[1]

A point which calls for notice is the further difficulty of deciding what we ought to mean by a single
sensum.   Physiologically we may be able to define it
as being the response of a single pressure spot or a
single temperature spot to a stimulus that does not
spread on to neighbouring spots.   But in the case of
all ordinary tactual experiences a large number, not
only of pressure-sensa, but also simultaneously of
temperature-sensa, are aroused.[2]   And it is in connection with this multiplicity of simultaneous sensa,
coming from different though usually neighbouring
locations, that space-perception takes place.   When
an ' isolated ' sensum is experimentally produced in the
psychological laboratory, it is being produced in a

---

[1] Cf. below, p. 214, passage quoted from Dr. Head.
[2] Cf. Dr. Head in *Brain*, vol. xli. p. 183.

percipient whose acquired powers of spatial discrimination and location are already highly developed, and who cannot therefore be sure that with the best intentions, and after every effort, he can succeed in divesting the sensum of all that does not intrinsically belong to it.　If, in addition, as even those who regard extensity as a property of all sensa usually agree in assuming, there be local-sign sensations which vary for each separate tactual spot, then even if a tactual sensum can be divested of all other external associations and accretions, it will still be accompanied by the corresponding local sign sensum; and it may be to the latter, not to the former, that extensity alone belongs. When, further, we bear in mind that the earlier experiences of touch, even when relatively precise and definite, have probably arisen, not primarily as perceptual localisations, but as reflex responses whereby bodily adjustment to the stimulus is automatically brought about with the least possible delay,[1] and that the tactual sensa have therefore always been accompanied by motor sensa, the part played by the tactual sensa, in and by themselves, is proportionately diminished.　Then, lastly, we have likewise to recognise that given sensa tend, as experience develops, to be vastly outnumbered by the previously experienced sensa which are recalled.[2]

When all these facts are taken into account, the two alternatives between which we have to choose become the plainer.　The sensa, given and recalled, as they thus multiply with the maturing of experience, do not remain unorganised.　So much is agreed.

---

[1] Cf. quotation from Mr. C. S. Myers, given below, pp. 211-12.

[2] Cf. Dr. Head on the part played by what he calls ' schemata,' *Brain*, vol. xxxiv. pp. 185-9.

Either, therefore, we must trace the sources of the organisation exclusively to the sensa, and so regard them as organising themselves through the mechanism of associative recall; and that will mean that we adopt the associationist view, that at each moment, and ever anew, the *entire* field, with all the complex factors of which it is made up, is reconstructed. Or else we hold that this applies only to the ever-changing sensory factors—certainly by themselves already sufficiently numerous and complex—and that the more constant factors, those which dictate the manner and method of organisation, and which in so doing voice the need for, and point the way towards, further advance, are otherwise provided for. The psychoplasm conceived on the analogy of the bioplasm will be, on this latter view, not a manifold of sensations, but a reacting agent with powers and capacities of a predetermined nature. Among these—only so is it a *psycho*plasm, and it is as legitimate to start in psychology from the fact of consciousness as in biology from the fact of life—must be the capacities which make possible awareness; and since a time-span and a space-extent are, as analysis of its maturer forms would seem to show, indispensable to its occurrence, these capacities must from the start allow of the apprehension of time and space, and therefore of the various formal factors necessary thereto. All these powers can be ascribed to the psychoplasm without our having to regard it as thereby approaching, still less outrivalling, the complexity of the bioplasm which organically conditions it. Taken together these predispositions will make possible that type of awareness to which I have given the title ' intuition,' meaning thereby the face to face apprehension of time and space.

(ii.) The Main Issue

But if neither time nor space be presented in the content of the given sensa, how, it will again be asked, is such apprehension possible? Upon this chief outstanding difficulty we may now at last venture a frontal attack.

By general admission, awareness is ultimate in the form of sensing. Thereby we acquire knowledge of a great variety of different types of existence—organic sensa, tastes, odours, pressures, temperatures, sounds, colours. The objection to our assuming that there is an equally ultimate process of intuiting is that the latter process never occurs save in terms of the former, and that when it does so, certain sensa themselves take on that very feature which, on our view, sensing is incapable of yielding. This objection is not merely that sensing will, at least so far as space is concerned, suffice to explain all our existing knowledge; but also that if sensa do *not* embody space, the process of intuition will be a process to which sensing does not serve as an analogy. For whereas the external world, through its action on the bodily senses, determines for the mind which of its multitudinous details will be attended to, there is (on the assumption of a non-sensory process of intuition) no corresponding machinery to provide for the confining of attention to this or that portion of space, and the shutting out of the two immensities (the great and the small) which engulf the mind when it attempts to contemplate space in its full actuality.

But this objection rests on the subjectivist assumption that sensa are in a quite different position from independent, physical existences. Virtually, it is being alleged that while it is understandable that the latter should exist in our close neighbourhood and yet not be known to us, sensa as ' in the mind ' must have free access to consciousness.   Now if we are really in earnest with the assertion that sensa are not mental states, but are objective happenings, and if we further recognise that they are not thereby cut off from being discovered by, and known to, the conscious mind, what objection can there be to our holding that time and space, which presumably are no less objective, are likewise apprehended in a direct manner?   We may take the absolute or the relational view of time and space.   Even on the absolute view they are relational modes of existence, at least to the extent of making possible certain unique types of relation between particular existences.   This I have recognised in the account which I have given of the nature of intuition. So far, then, sensing and intuiting—the differences which correspond to differences in their objects being thus allowed for—stand on the same level.   In both cases we *directly* apprehend the genuinely *objective*. And consequently the above-noted difficulty, that the process of apprehension is selective, and in all cases omits immensely more than it has knowledge of, applies equally to both.   Why we should be able to apprehend sensa, and yet be unable to apprehend those physiological processes which are, it would seem, their most immediate accompaniments, we are quite unable to say.   Usually, indeed, it is assumed that the processes of apprehension are effects of the processes in the brain, and that this sufficiently explains why the latter can never be themselves directly known.   Just because they are the means to, they can never themselves be the objects of the knowing process.   But this view, like the view of sensa as being ' in the mind,' commits us, I should maintain, to a subjectivist standpoint, and is therefore open to all those many objections which we have already considered. The problem of mind and brain cannot be disposed of in this easy, off-hand fashion, as if mind and brain were related in the same external manner as are causally connected processes in the physical world. I therefore feel justified in assuming that the limitation of sensing to the sensa that we at present have, is for us an ultimate fact which we have perforce to recognise, but which we cannot in any degree profess to explain. Presumably, the answer would involve such knowledge, not only of the nature and functioning of the brain, but also of the nature of mind, as is not yet even distantly foreshadowed in our present theories, even when most speculative.

But if this limitation whereby sensing has as its possible object, in this or that case, only this or that sensum, be allowed as ultimate, why should not a similar limitation be recognised in the case of intuiting? And if we take cognisance of the further fact, likewise vouched for by experience, that intuiting and sensing *mutually* condition one another, *neither* being possible in the absence of the other,[1] will not the uniformity of the limitation be as completely accounted for as the situation allows?

There will therefore remain to be considered only the one outstanding objection, that if sensa do not themselves possess extensity, there is no conceivable arrangement whereby they can come to be endowed with it. Is this objection conclusive? Does it suffice to show that we have been proceeding on false lines,

[1] Cf. pp. 82-3, 156-8, 182-3, 190-91.

and have here ended in an *impasse?*   My answer will be twofold.

In the first place, if we are justified in maintaining that time and space are beyond the scope of sensing in and by itself, then even if sensa are enduring and extended, their duration and extension will demand for their apprehension some such processes as those which we have ascribed to intuition.   In the second place, the sensa have hitherto been supposed to possess extension only on one or other of two assumptions. Either their extension is not that of the real world, but is proper to the sensa viewed as terminating members of lengthy series which begin by being physical and become physiological.   Or else their extension is independently real, and the so-called sensa are properties inherent in physical things.   The former view I reject because of the subjectivism with which it is bound up; and the latter because of its failure to account for the facts of perspective and illusion, and so for the very far-reaching differences between the world of ordinary consciousness and that of science. There therefore remains only the view which I have been advocating.   I may at once admit that I cannot, in any fully satisfactory manner, profess to explain how it comes about that in the combined action of sensing and intuiting the sensa are able to take on the spread-out form and the intuited space to become, what we have no evidence that it ever really is, warm or sonorous or coloured, and so in these respects sensible.   To this extent the objection will still, when all has been said, have to be recognised as a very serious, outstanding difficulty.   But, on the other hand, there are certain relevant and helpful considerations which, when borne in mind, have the effect of diminishing the force of the objection, and of suggesting possible lines upon which an answer compatible with the position here defended may ultimately be found. To these considerations, and to the very weighty corroborative evidence supplied by results recently obtained through physiological study of the brain, I shall now direct the reader's attention.

As we have noted,[1] there is a certain amount of empirical evidence that the intuitional factors, according as they take this or that form, determine what is actually seen, and not merely our judgments regarding what is seen. To employ our previous example, this is what happens in the case of the 'staircase' diagram; we can see it either as a staircase or as an overhanging cornice. Other examples [2] are the varying sizes of the sun and moon at the horizon, at their zenith, and as seen through a tube. These examples, it is true, cast no direct light upon the processes whereby extensionless sensa can have acquired extensity, but they may be interpreted as showing that the intuitional factors are at once relatively distinct from the sensory, and yet also extraordinarily influential in determining the latter. Though the amount of retinal stimulation is constant in the two cases, there is more spreadout colour when the moon is seen at the horizon than when it is seen in mid-heavens. Either this has to be admitted or we have to hold that the sensory field does not vary in size when on shipboard we look now down upon the deck and now out upon the sea and sky. Certainly, neither of the alternatives is an easy alternative. Either we have to question the possibility of variation in size, and that means likewise of depth, inde-

---

[1] Cf. above, p. 76 ff.   [2] Cf. above, p. 116 ff.

pendently of the amount of retina affected, and then set ourselves to deal with the many serious difficulties peculiar to such a view; or we recognise as one of the strange, but none the less certain, features of our sense-experience this extraordinary variability of visual fields, as contrasted with the relatively minute and absolutely fixed size of the retina,[1] and conclude therefrom that the intuitional factors, while capable of varying independently of the actual physical stimuli, are yet so closely concatenated with the sensory qualities as to determine the amounts of space over which these latter are apprehended as spreadout.

Further, since a close connection between sensa and extensity must, on any theory, be recognised as having been established at a very early stage, we are not required to assume that the various qualitative differences are developed prior to their being apprehended as spreadout. Since the general sensitiveness of the skin precedes the development of the senses of sight and hearing, the connection between sensa and extensity will presumably begin on the thermal and tactual levels. Thus if the eye in its origin be, as

---

[1] Cf. Sherrington, *The Integrative Action of the Nervous System*, p. 334 : " In the case of the eye not only is the slice of environment pertaining to it at even a short distance more wide and high than that of the skin, but it is at each moment multiplied by the third dimension. . . . In the photo-receptive system the so-called ' optic nerve ' (which, since it is the second neural link and therefore to some extent a ' common path,' presents numerical reduction from the first or private path in the retina itself) contains more conductive channels (nerve-fibres) in man (1,000,000, Krause) than are contained in the whole series of afferent spinal roots of one side of the body put together (634,000, Ingbert), and of these latter the cutaneous afferent fibres form only a part, and of that part the tango-receptive fibres themselves form only a fraction. The large number of the channels in the retinal path is no doubt primarily indicative of spatial differentiations of the receptive surface, but that spatial differentiation is itself indicative of the numbers of the stimuli frequenting that receptive field."

Dr. Sherrington declares,[1] simply "a set of glorified heat spots," which, owing to a lowering of the threshold of sensibility, have ceased to respond to heat-waves and now respond to the shorter and more delicate light-waves, the continuity of development will be assured, even at the critical stage at which the qualitative differences of light and colour begin to emerge. The connection established between thermal sensa and extension will be carried over, to be confirmed and extended in the newer visual experiences. For the heat-spots, however ' glorified,' will retain those brain-connections through which in their earlier functionings they have conditioned awareness of the locality affected, or at least have conditioned the reflex responses that vary with such localisation. As Mr. C. S. Myers has pointed out:

---

[1] *Op. cit.* p. 323 : " In the animal's progression certain of its segments *lead.* . . . [These] are exposed to external influences more than the rest. Not only do they receive *more* stimuli, meet *more* ' objects ' demanding pursuit or avoidance, but it is they which usually *first* encounter the agents beneficial or hurtful of the environment as related to the individual. Pre-eminent advantage accrues if the receptors of these segments react sensitively and differentially. . . . Some of them are specialised in such degree as almost obscures their fundamental affinity to others distributed in other segments. Thus among the system of receptors for which radiation is the adequate agent, there are developed in one of the leading segments a certain group, the *retinal,* particularly and solely, and extraordinarily highly, amenable to radiations of a certain limited range of wave-length. These are *photo-receptors,* for which light and only light, *e.g.* not heat, is the adequate stimulus. In like manner a certain group belonging to the system receptive of mechanical impacts attains such susceptibility for these as to react to the vibrations of water and air that constitute physical sounds. The retina is thus a group of glorified ' warmspots,' the cochlea a group of glorified ' touch-spots.' Again a group belonging to the system adapted to chemical stimuli reach in one of the leading segments such a pitch of delicacy [likewise through a lowering of the threshold of sensibility] that particles in quantity unweighable by the chemist, emanating from substances called odorous, excite reaction from them " [*i.e.* smell is taste at a distance : no odorous substance is, it appears, tasteless].

" A sweet taste corresponds with one type of reaction, a bitter taste with another; similarly with the sensations of colour and pitch, different types of reaction are evoked from longer or shorter waves. . . . At bottom, differences in type of movement must be the cause of differentiation in the quality of sensation; it would be of no advantage for the organism to experience different qualities of sensation, unless those differences were serviceable in promoting different types of response." [1]

Whatever readjustment and further elaboration of the intuitional machinery may be demanded before vision can discharge its present complex functions, there is no need of our assuming that the problem is to give spreadout form to sensa which first arise in complete independence as purely qualitative. What *is* alone essential is that we should recognise the distinct functions which sensing and intuiting, and also therefore the corresponding types of brain-processes, are called upon to discharge, and the fact that both are required to make possible sense-experience of the kind possessed by us.[2]

A similar explanation can be given why sounds should tend to be apprehended as having a " roominess." If the ear be " a set of glorified touch-spots," the auditory sensa, in the stage, so to speak, before they have themselves come about, will have acquired

[1] Quoted by Alexander, *Space, Time and Deity*, vol. ii. p. 128, from *Brit. Journal of Psychology*, vol. vi., ii. § 1. Cf. also Head, *Brain*, vol. xli. (1918), p. 184 (*Studies in Neurology*, pp. 746-7).

[2] Cf. Alexander, *Space, Time and Deity*, vol. ii. p. 148: " In sensing a colour we have not two separate acts of consciousness whose objects we refer to one another. There is no separate *consciousness* of the place, to which to refer the colour; for the consciousness or intuition of the place is only excited so far as we have the sense of the colour. . . . Consequently there are not two acts of mind but only one act of mind, which in its sensory character apprehends the colour, and in its intuitive character apprehends the place of it. We are conscious of a place coloured or of colour in a place."

that relation to space which is usual in tactual sensa. In this case, however, the connection established on the tactual level has, for obvious reasons, not been so strongly reinforced as in the case of sight. Indeed we may rather regard it as having continued only in a weakened and faded-out form.

These remarks, as I recognise, only suffice to throw the difficulty further back. How come extensionless, thermal and tactual sensa to acquire the spreadout form? If the problem cannot be answered on the visual level, neither can it be answered on the more primitive levels. What alone has been gained is an appreciation of the gradual manner in which our present experiences have been brought about, and consequently of the complexity of the processes which at the innumerable intermediate stages have presumably been at work; and this forms a natural bridge, over which we can pass to consideration of the very revolutionary results obtained by Dr. Head and his collaborators, in their investigations into the physiological conditions of the cutaneous sensations. Hitherto I have intentionally avoided all reference to these important results, partly because the positions which I am maintaining had been arrived at before the work of Dr. Head and his collaborators had come to my attention,[1] and my general argument would only have been obscured by their earlier introduction, and partly because, in physiological investigations of so difficult and complicated a character, the results reached, though in certain respects sufficiently definite,

[1] I must previously have read the Supplementary Note in Mr. Alexander's *Space, Time and Deity*, vol. ii. p. 178, in which Dr. Head's work is referred to, but evidently then failed to appreciate its real character and importance. I first read Dr. Head's articles in *Brain* in the summer of 1923, while I was revising this chapter.

are still much too tentative to serve as basis for a philosophical analysis of sense-experience. A brief statement of them may, however, serve to show that the most recent developments in the physiology of the brain are very decidedly pointing in the direction of some such position as I have been outlining.

Take, for instance, the naïve, traditional assumption that the impulses which originate in peripheral end-organs " pass unaltered to the cortex, there to underlie that psychical state we call a sensation." [1] This assumption, Dr. Head maintains, is no longer tenable.

" The day of the *a priori* psychologist is over so far as sensation is concerned. A man can no longer sit in his study and spin out of himself the laws of psychology by a process of self-examination. For we have been able to show that, at a level deeper than any he can reach by introspection, are prepared those states which condition the nature and characteristics of the ultimate sensation. Appreciation of position in space, graduated response to stimuli of varying intensity, and recognition of the similarity and difference of objects in contact with the body, were all thought to be matters of ' judgment.' We have shown that the forms assumed by these aspects of sensation are ordered and predestined on the physiological level, as the result of innumerable integrations, which take place outside consciousness. These processes are not open to conscious analysis; it is only the interplay of sensations that can be discovered by introspection." [2]

Broadly stated, Dr. Head's main conclusion is that apprehension of cutaneous sensations, on their qualitative side, is distinct from apprehension of their localities

---

[1] *Brain*, vol. xxxiv., 1911–12, p. 182 (*Studies in Neurology*, pp. 601-2); cf. vol. xli., 1918, p. 177: " The psychologist, who attempts to discover a strict psychophysical parallelism, ignores the central link of the problem. He assumes that the nature and conditions of the physical stimulus can be brought into direct relation with the psychical act of sensation."

[2] *Loc. cit.* vol. xli. p. 177 (*Studies in Neurology*, p. 741).

in the body and of their positions relatively to one
another. He cites evidence to show that the optic
thalamus is the organ which conditions sensations of
pain, the crude sensations of heat and cold, and the
sensations of contact and roughness. When through
brain-lesions the thalamus acts independently of the
cerebral cortex, these sensations are experienced
merely in their affective and qualitative aspects, without
precise spatial discrimination of any kind.

" The patient generally gives up all attempts at appreciation,
saying he has ' no idea ' of the shape, form, or relative size and
weight of the test-object." [1] " A cortical lesion never abolishes
sensibility to contact; the response may be intermittent,
irregular, and grossly defective, but is never completely absent.
A weight resting on the hand may not be recognised, but at
the moment when it is placed on the skin and, not infrequently,
when it is removed, or even gently touched, the patient says
that ' something has happened.' When the loss of sensation is
extremely severe and all sensory impulses passing to the cortex
have been cut off, the patient may be unable to recognise that
the effect he experiences is produced by an external object and
may simply reply that something is happening to him. These
contact-stimuli, which may produce this vague sensation of
' something happening ' within the body, evoke precise recognition that an object is acting on its surface when the cortical
paths are intact." [2]

On Dr. Head's view, the afferent impulses which
pass to the optic thalamus, and under normal conditions
from the thalamus to the cortex, are in all cases highly
complex. So far from standing in direct, simple
correlation with the physical stimulus, they are sufficiently numerous and diverse to form five distinct sets
of impulses, each set following its own path, and each

[1] *Brain*, vol. xxxiv. p. 185 (*Studies in Neurology*, p. 604).
[2] *Loc. cit.* vol. xxxiv. p. 181 (*Studies in Neurology*, pp. 600-601).

therefore liable to be separately affected by brain-lesions. The respective functions of these five sets of afferent impulses are, he maintains,[1] as follows: (1) to yield the appreciation of postural position and passive movement; (2) to facilitate the discrimination and recognition of tactile qualities other than contact and roughness, and the discrimination of differences in weight; (3) to condition spatial discrimination and the recognition of size and shape; (4) to make possible localisation of a spot affected; (5) to yield discrimination of thermal sensations and recognition of their variations in intensity. That is to say, Dr. Head is prepared to argue, in view of the pathological phenomena which follow upon nervous lesions and of other evidence, that all forms of spatial apprehension are independent of touch, being conditioned by brain-arrangements distinct from those which condition the strictly qualitative differences.

" When the influence of the cortex is removed, and the optic thalamus exerts its activity uncontrolled, the patient may cease to associate his sensory experiences with any external agency. Removal of the cortical factors in sensation has reduced to elementary proportions the power of projection, as we know it in the intact human being. It is no longer possible to recognise the size, shape, weight, and spatial relations of an external object, nor, indeed, to appreciate the relative intensity of the stimulating action it excites." [2]

In the development of the higher centres the thalamus has, of course, been brought into subordination to the cortex.

" All stimuli which appeal to the thalamic centre have a high threshold. They must reach a high intensity before they

---

[1] *Brain*, vol. xxxiv. p. 183 (*Studies in Neurology*, p. 602).
[2] *Loc. cit.* vol. xli. pp. 188-9 (*Studies in Neurology*, pp. 750-51).

can enter consciousness, but once they have risen above the threshold they tend to produce a change of excessive amount and duration, and this it is the business of the cortical mechanism to control. The low intensity of the stimuli that can arouse the sensory cortex, and its quick reaction-period, enable it to control the activity of the cumbersome mechanism of the thalamic centre." [1]

But, as Dr. Head adds, we must not expect to experience, even in the abnormal conditions caused by brain-lesions, the original crude experiences of the earlier stage.

" The functions of the central nervous system are not a palimpsest where a new text is written over an earlier manuscript partly erased. The more primitive activities have been profoundly modified by the advent of the new centres, which utilise some of the faculties originally possessed by the older mechanism." " Removal of [the] dominant mechanism does not reveal the functions of the phylogenetically older organs in all their primary simplicity. The original thalamencephalon contained elements, not only of the human optic thalamus, but also, in a crude form, of certain physiological processes, now entirely relegated to the cerebral cortex. Even the specific activity of this original thalamus was incomparably less highly developed than the dissociated thalamic functions of man. . . . A lesion which sets free the human optic thalamus . . . reveals a condition, which is a part of the complete [later developed] act and does not reproduce an ancient mechanism in its original form." [2]

Dr. Head outlines, in terms of motor response, an alternative method of distinguishing between sub-cortical and cortical functions. Segmented animals respond to stimuli by co-ordinated movements leading to retraction of the segment affected. A higher

---

[1] *Brain*, vol. xxxiv. p. 191 (*Studies in Neurology*, p. 609).
[2] *Loc. cit.* vol. xli. pp. 182, 180 (*Studies in Neurology*, pp. 745, 743-4).

development of function in the central nervous system makes possible the more complicated mass-reflex, whereby local defensive retraction is replaced by movements of the whole animal. Both these types of response are, however, of an uncontrolled character. Only when, in those still higher types of animal life in which the leading segment, that which normally first advances into new territory, assumes dominance by becoming the seat of the " distance receptors," such as the olfactory epithelium, the hair-cells of the ear, and the pigment spots of the eye, does discriminative choice make its appearance, and the resulting motor responses become genuinely adaptive and selective in character.[1] In one respect all three types of response agree, namely, in that the character of the response varies independently of the quality of the stimulus, in correlation with the position of the part affected. " Scratching the sole of the foot is followed by a different movement from that caused by stimulating [in the same manner] the skin of the thigh." [2] Accordingly in all three types we have to assume the existence of afferent impulses distinct from those of the special senses. The adaptive type of response differs, however, in quite radical fashion from the other two, in that it involves *conscious awareness* of space. For

---

[1] Cf. Sherrington, *The Integrative Action of the Nervous System*, pp. 335-6 : " The animal's receptive range . . . is greater in the direction about the ' leading ' pole. . . . The visual receptors are usually near the leading pole, and so placed that they see into the field whither progression goes. And similarly with the olfactory receptors. The motor train behind, the elongated motor machinery of the rest of the body [the fore and aft arrangement of the lower vertebrates] is therefore from this point of view a motor appendage at the behest of the distance-receptor organs in front. The segments lying at the leading pole of the animal, armed as they are with the great ' distance ' sense-organs, constitute what is termed the ' head.' "

[2] *Brain*, vol. xli. p. 189 (*Studies in Neurology*, p. 751).

though the motor response is still, of course, executed through reflex mechanisms, it is so highly discriminative, in delicately varied adaptation to *objective* relations, that merely qualitative, affective experiences no longer suffice.[1]   There is demanded a capacity for apprehending " complex projectional relations," *i.e.* a public world in space and time.   Segmental and massive responses yield only automatic withdrawal from noxious influences.   Adaptive action, consciously directed in view of a spatially ordered environment, alone makes possible manipulative control over the external agencies.

" When we attempt to climb through barbed wire, we are forced to respond not only to the pain but to the position of the wire.   The pain produced by pricking a protopathic hand is all-compelling; it is impossible not to make a movement of withdrawal.   But under normal conditions the ungovernable reaction is controlled by the existence of those forms of sensibility which underlie recognition of relations in space.   This enables us to choose whether the hand shall be removed or not. . . . Thus, it is essentially the spatial elements in sensory impressions which have led to the transformation of an inevitable segmental reaction into a discriminative response of the complete organism. . . . The projected aspects of sensation are not related to ourselves, but to external objects.   In fact, an ' object ' might be defined as a complex of projected responses; it is said to have characters, such as size, shape, weight, and position in space, which distinguish it from all others.   The recognition of such features, however, depends on physiological activities, the product of certain definite centres in the cortex. If these processes are unable to influence consciousness, the

---

[1] Cf. *loc. cit.* : " On the reflex level, afferent impulses can be shown to be adapted to spatial conditions and to the intensity and relative character of the stimulus, although the whole procedure remains outside consciousness. If, however, they succeed in reaching the highest receptive centres, they endow sensation with spatial attributes, relative intensity, and individual character."

' object' disappears, although its affective and qualitative aspects still produce their appropriate sensory reactions." [1]

In this manner Dr. Head reinforces and further extends the views which Dr. Sherrington has so impressively developed in his *Integrative Action of the Nervous System*. The cerebral cortex being the organ not only of the distance-receptors—of smell, hearing, and sight—but also of the processes whereby the spatial features of these and all other sensa are apprehended, sensations which on the lower level, prior to cortical development, can possess, with any definiteness, the aspects only of quality and feeling-affection, then take on those ' projectional ' features which characterise our specifically human type of experience. And this view Dr. Head would still further extend, to cover our consciousness of time.

"The sensory activities of the cortex are not only responsible for projection in space, but also ensure recognition of sequence in time. . . . One of the commonest defects produced by a cortical injury is this want of temporal definition; a stimulus, rhythmically repeated, ' seems to be there all the time.' The patient cannot appreciate the moment at which it is applied or removed. There is no complete recognition of an extended sequence of events.

" Thus, it is the projected elements in sensation to which we owe our conceptions both of coherence in space and in time. I have attempted to show that these factors are not essentially due to judgment or conscious association, but depend to a great extent on physiological activities and dispositions. When these are permitted to excite consciousness, they appear as an ordered sensation, related to other events in the external world and extended serially in time." [2]

[1] *Brain*, vol. xli. pp. 191-2 (*Studies in Neurology*, pp. 753-4).
[2] *Loc. cit.* vol. xli. p. 193 (*Studies in Neurology*, p. 754). "All the higher projectional aspects of sensation . . . form a continuous series of dispositions. . . . The unit of consciousness, as far as these factors in sensation

This, as the reader will note, comes very near to a doctrine of temporal and spatial intuition. Though Dr. Head's investigations have, thus far, been directed almost exclusively to the cutaneous senses, analogous results would doubtless be obtained if a similar investigation could be made of the phenomena of vision. Since vision develops so much later, and would seem to be so much more dependent upon the hemispheres,[1] it is hardly likely that colours will ever be experienced, even in the most extensive brain-lesions, save in the spreadout form. This, however, is only what we should expect if Dr. Head is justified in his main contention as to the manner in which sensation is complexly conditioned at a lower level than any to which introspection can penetrate.[2] The terms ' projected ' and ' projectional ' are, I should maintain, unnecessarily subjectivist in character, and indeed derive from the psychology which Dr. Head is so effectively undermining. Dr. Head has himself, however, made it amply clear that he does not mean to suggest that sensations are first apprehended as unprojected, and are projected by some subsequent mental process.

" Those factors in sensation do not depend primarily on ' judgment ' or ' association '; for, on the physiological level, afferent impulses possess projectional characteristics." [3]

Such, then, is the empirical evidence in support of the distinction between sensing and intuiting. As

are concerned, is not a moment of time, but a ' happening.' This consists of a group of occurrences belonging to profoundly different orders in the psycho-physiological hierarchy."

[1] Cf. Sherrington, *Integrative Action of the Nervous System*, pp. 335, 349, 390.

[2] Cf. the passage quoted above, p. 214.

[3] *Brain*, vol. xli. p. 189 (*Studies in Neurology*, p. 751).

already stated, I have no desire to suggest that this evidence can be interpreted only in this one way, as favouring the precise doctrines which I have been defending.   It can, however, at least be argued that not only are these doctrines quite as compatible with the physiological and other evidence as are the counter-views, but that they have the great advantage of allowing us to regard our knowledge as being of independent reality, and as sufficiently reliable to permit of a progressively deepening scientific insight into its absolute nature.   For though I have gone so far with the subjectivists as to allow that in locating the secondary qualities in physical objects we are, almost certainly, subject to an illusion, these qualities are on our theory aids to the discrimination of the *real* position, *real* shape, and *real* motion of bodies, and need not, therefore, prevent our regarding sense-experience as being the direct apprehension, however partial and distorted, of a real and independent material world.   The extensity apprehended *in terms of* sensa is the extensity of the perceived objects, not of the sensa as such.

If some such realist view, after due weight has been allowed to all the relevant considerations, proves to be, on the whole, the most satisfactory interpretation of the cognitive situation, need we be driven out of it by those objections which we have been considering? In view of the present infant stage of psychology, of our very imperfect knowledge of the brain, and of the very incomplete analysis yet made of our fundamental categories, and perhaps not least of the baffling character of time and space, which have not yet yielded all their secrets even to the mathematician, any theory of knowledge is bound to be highly conjectural and tentative.   Every type of philosophy has to be allowed some freedom in the choice of its difficulties as well as of its strong points, and so in deciding in its various fields for that theory which proves most helpful in dealing with the broader issues. If subjectivism proves more hampering than helpful as a general philosophical standpoint, the many doubtful features in a realist view, provided these be not demonstrably incompatible with the doctrines avowed or with the ascertainable data, are no sufficient reason for regarding it as untenable.

CHAPTER IX

CONCLUSIONS

I SHALL conclude by indicating, in a quite summary manner, the main consequences that follow upon adoption of the standpoint which I have been advocating.

In substituting for Dr. Head's general distinction between crude and projected sensation several more special distinctions, I have ascribed to the brain-processes a complexity even greater than that which he has depicted. On the view above presented, the cerebral processes conditioning our human sense-experience will consist in the concatenated interplay, on the one hand, of the three types of processes which condition sensing, intuiting, and categorial thinking, and, on the other hand, of these three types of processes with those other processes which condition the sensa. On the mental side, brain-development will thus be accompanied by a steadily increasing enlargement and articulation of the world directly experienced, and by a correspondingly increased complexity in the cognitive processes whereby it is enabled, in this degree, to reveal itself to us. This does not, of course, bring us any nearer to a solution of the problem in what manner precisely the mind is conditioned (or it may be liberated) by the body; but at least, if my analysis of sense-experience be in general correct, we have secured direct apprehension—foreshortened, indeed, and as we may say ' glorified,' in terms of sensa, but still none the less direct apprehension—of the independently real; and have done so without making any assumptions beyond what the empirical data would seem to justify.

Since categories are in all cases purely formal, only by empirical study can we obtain insight into the nature of the existences to which they apply. Thus we cannot hope to determine in any *a priori* manner, or by any kind of dialectical argument, that the self is a unity or is ' self-subsistent.' On these questions the empirical data are alone competent to determine our conclusions, and are of a very varied nature, partly sensory, partly spiritual, derived from all the diverse, relevant fields. For in dealing with the self, our attention must not be limited to introspective study of our so-called inner states and processes, nor even to study of these in their connection with the brain. Owing to the obvious manner in which so much else than the brain co-operates with it in the production of sensa, the brain is universally recognised as integral to nature; but the self, even apart from all relation to the brain, is integral to nature in a still more fundamental manner. Since awareness presupposes, for its very existence, an objective field, and since this field—if our view be correct—has as its most fundamental features real, independent time and space, the relation of mind and nature is, as we must recognise, a problem much more comprehensive than any dealt with in the current theories of the relation of mind and body. And when to these conditions we add the values which elicit our energies and direct our activities, to the consequent transformation of the

Q

given environment, as also of the self, perspectives, yet wider in character, open to our view. As Whitehead justly remarks [1]—though in a somewhat different connection—the ignoring of these and other relevant facts has

" been disastrous both to science and to philosophy, but chiefly to philosophy. It has transformed the grand question of the relations between nature and mind into the petty form of the interaction between the human body and mind." " Knowledge is ultimate. There can be no explanation of the ' why ' of knowledge; we can only describe the ' what ' of knowledge. . . . The object of . . . metaphysical science is not to explain knowledge, but to exhibit in its utmost completeness our concept of reality."

What, then, is the situation which our knowledge does actually disclose? What kind of world is revealed in sense-experience, and how does the self stand related to it? The world experienced is a single domain, complexly unified. As in space, its parts are in continuous connection with one another, and so in their ' totality ' form a single whole. As in time, its events stand in continuous temporal relations of past, present, and future, and so, from this point of view also, form a single whole. Again, as organised through the categories of substance, causality, and reciprocity, it forms a dynamically interconnected system. And since time and space are its fundamental and most pervasive features, continuity may be described as its primary characteristic.

Accordingly I have adopted Ward's doctrine of a presentational continuum, while modifying it in one fundamental respect. Ward's position is as thoroughgoing in its subjectivism as is the teaching of Leibniz,

[1] *The Concept of Nature*, pp. 27 ff., 31-2.

with which in other respects his philosophy has so many points of contact. The continuum is, he maintains, a *sensory* field private to each percipient. In opposition to this view I am maintaining what would appear to be essential to any genuinely realistic standpoint, that what is strictly sensory in the continuum is not continuous, and that what is continuous in it is not sensory. So far as time and space are concerned, the outer world presents itself to us directly, as it were in its own person. Time and space in their inexhaustiveness [1]—the feature which renders continuity the source of all the problems of infinitude— bear the imprint of reality, and fecundate the mind as nothing else does. In the process of getting itself into consciousness the outer world has, indeed, become deprived of all but a very small portion of its rich content, and what remains is altered and simplified in terms of the sensa which it brings into existence through its action upon the living organism. It presents to us only such of its features as we must have cognisance of, if, as animal existences, we are to adapt ourselves to them. More would be useless, and as preoccupying the mind positively harmful. And in order that the adaptive processes may be sufficiently rapid and effective, these selected features are also presented in a perspective which is unique and personal.

When these allowances are made, little may seem to be left that is genuinely public. Nothing that we experience exists independently, precisely in the form in which we experience it. So far we can agree with the subjectivists. Indeed, since imagination is tied

[1] Cf. Whitehead, *The Concept of Nature*, p. 14: " Unexhaustiveness is an essential characteristic of our knowledge of nature."

down to the secondary qualities, we have to admit that while the independent constitution of objects may be conceptually apprehended in the light of the results established by the sciences, such concepts can never be rendered precise through the employment of images. For though the independently real is tasted, smelt, and touched, and is apprehended through its radiations of sound, temperature, and light, we have no means of determining how far, or in what manner, any of these qualities may precisely match those with which it is intrinsically endowed. Even the primary qualities are not apprehended in any quite impersonal manner. The maximum field which a blind man can sensuously experience at first hand, at any one moment, consists in the space which he spans with outstretched arms. This is not, indeed, for the blind man, a fixed unit, determined by the length of his arms. In so far as it is three-dimensional it is highly elastic. If what he thus grasps is, say, the corner of a house, he directly experiences a space very much larger than the extent of his grasp. Still in the case of the blind man, immediate experiences of this character are the only data at his disposal when he endeavours to conceive imaginatively the vast spaces of geography and astronomy. The power of sight enables us to envisage a wider simultaneous whole; for though the eye be so much smaller than the hand, and minute compared with the outstretched arms,[1] yet, thanks to the meanings with which visual space is saturated, we find its field to be now a few cubic inches, now an open landscape, now the boundless ocean or the starry heavens. But all such immediately experienced spaces, whether of the blind or of the seeing, fail to do justice to what

---

[1] Cf. passage quoted from Dr. Sherrington above, p. 210 *n.*

is being apprehended. Since space is continuous, even the smallest area is itself an immensity relatively to its parts; and consequently its size as experienced, whether in perception or in imagination, can never be true to the 'absolute scale' (whatever that may mean) of its object, be it large or small. In picturing a molecule or the Western Hemisphere we represent them by the device of some convenient unit (arbitrary save in its determination by practical considerations) that scales up the almost incredible minuteness of structure in the molecule, and scales down the vast regions of the two Americas. And just as in the case of the molecule we have to omit most of the detail of its atomic and sub-atomic structure, so in the case of the Americas we have to leave out of the reckoning the houses, the boundaries and shapes of fields—indeed all but a quite minute proportion of the constituent features.

But when all such considerations have been allowed their full weight, it remains true that as regards the consequences which follow, there is an all-important difference between a subjectivist theory and the thesis here propounded. If what we experience is in *any* degree and respect public and not private, independently real and not merely subjective, then, however partially and distortedly it is apprehended, we may by indirection find in its appearances data sufficient for its truer apprehension. And this indeed is, as I have already remarked, in many respects the most surprising feature of the whole strange situation. Nature, in determining the character of the animal organism, of its sense-organs and nervous system generally, has had in view primarily only the self-preservation of the species. Yet in following this path, she has also made possible the acquiring of knowledge. In preparing such knowledge as is of aid in survival—allowing no more knowledge than is indispensable for this purpose—she has in man brought into existence, or at least liberated, a type of sense-experience which, when reinforced by instruments of precision, when sifted and tested by all manner of indirect experimental devices, yields data sufficient for the attaining of scientific insight. What has been evolved under the apparently exclusive domination of purely practical needs, turns out in the end to subserve, with amazing adequacy, the requirements of the disinterested seeker after truth.

This is the supreme example of Nature's many-sidedness. Nature creates beauty as widespread as herself, while in the process, as it would appear, attending only to strictly utilitarian ends. That insects and other animals may have food, and that plants may scatter their seed, she develops the flowers and the fruits, with all their diversity of pleasing form, scent, and colouring. But in no field does Nature succeed in bringing down two such different birds with a single stone as in human sense-experience, so elaborately arrived at by way of the sense-organs and nervous system. Nature here set out to devise methods whereby the most rudimentary organisms may secure a sufficiency of food and maintain themselves and the species in a not over-promising environment. She struggled with this problem for millions of years, and what is very admirable—we can hardly help personifying Nature; we obtain so versatile and intriguing a personality when we do—is that no sooner had she solved her initial problem than she contrived to complicate it by making the organisms which she had thus successfully equipped improve themselves into beings that demanded a wider environment and a fresh equipment. And this went on, the first solutions being modified and elaborated so as to cover new factors, until, after well-nigh interminable intermediate stages, she has as her supreme invention the nervous system of the higher vertebrates. And what then follows surpasses in strangeness all that has gone before. All along Nature has, seemingly, been intent upon providing her creatures, in their conscious experience, with an adequate instrument of practical adaptation. And now we find that while successfully doing this, she has at the same time, as it were inadvertently, provided the last-born of her children with the means of setting aside all immediate practical purposes, and indeed of establishing himself in her ancient rights, taking the future into his own hands, and deliberately thwarting her when her ways do not conform to his own preferred plans. Discerning truth, beauty, and goodness, he adopts the attitude of contemplation, and in view of these absolute values organises even his practical life on a different plane.

But this surely is a perverse and unconvincing view of the situation thus disclosed. Can Nature's proceedings be so purely accidental as this account of them would imply? Is it not truer—keeping merely to the bare facts—to reverse the point of view, and to recognise as supremely significant the seemingly accidental bye-products of Nature's animal devices? Nature—such, at least, has been her actual behaviour —seeks man out; she creates him, endows him with theoretical as well as with other needs, and then progressively responds to these needs, the more he seeks her aid. Is not Nature here revealing herself—I raise the question, but shall not attempt to discuss it —as Super-Nature; and can she be synoptically envisaged save when so conceived? [1]

And is not this view—it is the idealist view—alone truly realistic? It enables us to regard Nature as integrally bound up with the conditions that make knowledge possible. Nature, while occupied in bringing about the animal organism, has likewise, throughout the whole process, been engaged in bringing about the knowing mind, and in responding to the faculties with which she endows it. Furthermore, in endowing man with those instinctive, emotional needs which finally develop into intellectual curiosity and the passionate ambition to discover truth, she has also contrived to provide him with the necessary driving power that enables her, working from her own side, to make her revelation of herself to him more and more complete. Nature has sought out man, has come to him, has stimulated, aroused, and possessed him; and in all his conscious experience her continuous co-operation is the primary condition of his ever-increasing success.

A subjectivist view of knowledge, we may therefore maintain, is not merely inadequate; it is a complete misreading of the actual facts. In interpreting the situation through its subjectivist features, it renders unintelligible the objective factors, which, however obscured by perspective, play a quite fundamental rôle in shaping and determining the possibility and the growth of knowledge. From the start, in the awareness of time and space, and therefore in

---

[1] Treatment of this question does not come within the scope of the present volume. That would involve discussion of the various problems bearing upon the reality and *prevenient* influence of spiritual values.

some manner and degree of the categories, reality has secured direct representation in the field of consciousness, and in so doing has *imposed* upon the mind an objective interpretation of its private sensa, opening, even to the view of the animal mind, a public world in which it meets its fellows face to face—so much so that even for man the discovery that his world is not wholly public, but in its features largely determined by perspective in terms of sensa, is itself one of the later results of theoretical inquiry.

Such, then, would seem to be the character of the world experienced, and such has been its actual, historical behaviour, in preparing the physical and physiological conditions in and through which our sense-experience and our scientific knowledge have come about. How, now, does the situation appear when we view it from the other end, namely, from the point of view of the knowing mind? In answer to this question, I have mainly dwelt upon one all-important consideration. Though the self may—as an idealist, I believe that it does—possess powers which in certain respects transcend the strictly natural, yet, as we learn from experience, such powers are capable of acting only in so far as Nature affords not only the opportunities but also the terms and material required for their effective operation.[1] This is most strikingly obvious in that feature through which, more than through any other, the mind transcends the given and immediate, and in which, indeed, all its metaphysical needs have their source, namely, in its apprehension of totality and infinitude. This power of transcendence is the mind's own power, but it is

---

[1] Cf. Baron F. von Hügel, *The Mystical Element of Religion* (2nd edition, 1923), vol. i. pp. 43-7 ; vol. ii. p. 367 ff.

assisted and *constrained* thereto by the essential features of the time and the space which characterise Nature in those of its aspects which would seem to be most completely, and—if mistakenly interpreted on subjectivist, Cartesian lines — even to be dualistically opposed to the mental processes whereby they are apprehended.   Accordingly, when these and the other kindred considerations, which we have already noted, are borne in mind, whatever other issues may remain for discussion, we should at least be under no temptation to seek solution of the problems of philosophy in any such easy fashion as may seem to offer when we do violence to the unity of Nature by treating mind and matter as separate, self-conditioned existences, standing in merely external, causal relations to one another.   We shall agree with the extreme materialistic type of naturalism—as against the dualistic or agnostic types so favoured in the nineteenth century —at least in this, that we find no grounds for believing that there are separate sovereignties in the Universe, standing in external, and so to speak diplomatic or hostile, intercourse with one another.   There is ample scope—in proportion as evidence is forthcoming—for distinguishing between the inorganic and the organic, between the physical and the mental, between the natural and the spiritual; but in these distinctions we shall not expect to find separable factors.   The organic, for instance, does not exist apart from the inorganic, but consists in the raising of the latter to higher powers.   What we shall look for are different levels wherein the lower yields embodiment to the higher, and the higher by means of the lower achieves that which is proper to itself.   Such contentions appear to be in harmony with, or at least not to be incompatible with, the known facts; and at the same time they have the very considerable recommendation that they are more in keeping with our abysmal ignorance of the other, yet unknown, possibilities of which reality may permit, than are the counter-views that rest upon dualistic distinctions which for their establishment demand knowledge beyond what we possess.

We shall also conclude that the distinction between appearance and reality (phenomena and things in themselves), however applied, is quite peculiarly un-fitted to express the relation between mind and Nature. The mind does, indeed, condition the possibility of appearance. Appearance is a simplification of reality, demanded for the purposes of animal and human existence.[1] In the achievement of this goal, the sensa, as so many real happenings, come about, and form an important addition to the sum of reality. In and through them Nature manifests its power of "creatively advancing into novelty." Considered simply as occurrences, and apart from the uses for which we

---

[1] So far I can agree with Mr. G. Dawes Hicks that "the distinction between a 'thing' and its 'appearances' is *not* a distinction between the 'thing' as a whole and its constituents. A 'thing' is made up of parts and of qualities, and any one of its qualities may 'appear' in a countless number of ways. But this quality is not resolvable into its ways of appearing; it remains one, though its appearances vary, and is, as such, a quality of the 'real thing,' while the appearances of it are not. The appearances are no more than the orderly manner in which the quality is apprehended by a finite mind under the conditions and limitations imposed by sense intuition" (*Proc. Arist. Soc.*, 1916–17, pp. 357-8). Cf. also *Proc.* for 1913–1914, p. 27: "The antithesis which continually besets our thinking between things as they are and things as they appear is not an antithesis between two separate spheres of existence. Things as they appear are not external to or independent of things as they are; things as they are *do* appear. . . . The contrast falls within experience itself and in no way points beyond it."

employ them, they are not appearances but realities. Furthermore, they enable reality, working through man, to add to itself, by creation of the manual and of the fine arts, types of being different from any that ' naturally ' exist. But in these activities, as in those of ordinary experience and of science, mind does *not* fall on the side of appearance; it reveals to us both reality and appearance, enabling us to draw the distinction and increasingly to discern, and in theory to correct, the illusions through which appearances fulfil their practical ends. Appearance connects with *practical* ends, and with the limitation of outlook necessary for concentration, and for rapidity and ease of response. Mind, as standing for *theoretical* values, is the great emancipator from the illusions which thus result. Knowledge, to repeat, is *knowledge*; its function is to reveal; it is not creative, but contemplative. Even when what we contemplate is, as we say, ' only appearance,' as when we see an object behind a mirror, what is so perceived reduces without remainder, alike as regards its sensed and its intuited factors, to the actually existent. The exigencies of practical life have intervened, through induced habits and other means that may perhaps be partly physiological, and if mental are certainly non-conscious, to determine ' incorrect ' location, as well as simplification and perspective in terms of sensa; but the last named, the sensa, are real events, integral to Nature; and the former are non-conscious processes whose occurrence we can learn to appreciate, and in theory to discount.

Since, then, appearance has a practical use, and therefore normally a sufficient reason for existing, it casts no doubt upon the general reliability of our mental processes, or upon their capacity, when we use the resources placed at our disposal, progressively to penetrate to the absolutely real. The knowing mind is able to do so, not because it is independent of the world which it apprehends, but because it is integrally bound up with it, and so is ministered to and upheld by it. More problems remain than are hereby answered. But at least we are assured of one all-important conclusion. Since reality lies open to our view, it can be relied upon, as we extend the range of our empirical data, sensory and spiritual, and interpret them by the aid of theories rigorously tested, to educate us ever more fully into understanding of itself.

INDEX

Printed in Great Britain by R. & R. CLARK, LIMITED, *Edinburgh.*